Risk Communication

The Conservation Foundation

Board of Directors

The Conservation Foundation is a nonprofit research and communications organization dedicated to encouraging human conduct to sustain and enrich life on earth. Since its founding in 1948, it has attempted to provide intellectual leadership in the cause of wise management of the earth's resources. The Conservation Foundation is affiliated with World Wildlife Fund.

Risk Communication

Proceedings of the
National Conference on Risk Communication,
held in Washington, D.C.,
January 29-31, 1986

Edited by J. Clarence Davies, Vincent T. Covello,
and Frederick W. Allen

 The Conservation Foundation
Washington, D.C.

Risk Communication

Cover design by Berns & Kay, Ltd., Bethesda, Maryland
Typography by Rings-Leighton, Ltd., Washington, D.C.
Printed by McNaughton & Gunn, Saline, Michigan

The Conservation Foundation
1250 Twenty-Fourth Street, N.W.
Washington, D.C. 20037

Library of Congress Cataloging in Publication Data
National Conference on Risk Communication (1986 : Washington, D.C.)
    Risk communication.

    Bibliography: p.
    1. Risk communication—Congresses. I. Davies, J. Clarence. II. Covello,
Vincent T. III. Allen, Frederick W. IV. Conservation Foundation. V. Title.
T10.68.N38   1986   363.1   87-27155
ISBN 0-89164-103-3

Contents

Foreword

Risk communication, until recently, has been a neglected topic. It was assumed that much of the conflict or confusion over risk questions was due to public ignorance, industry, duplicity, or bureaucratic indifference. Although it would be foolhardy to say that these kinds of factors are not sometimes important, a deeper understanding of the problems has revealed that often the communication process itself is either at fault or, at the least, exacerbates the problem. Risk communicators simply do not do a good job of getting their message across. Conflict and alienation are sharpened rather than reduced. The values and perceptions that the public brings to risk evaluation are ignored or misunderstood by the communicators, increasing the suspicions of the public and widening the gap between expert opinion and political reality.

This issue report is based on the presentations and discussions at the National Conference on Risk Communication, held in Washington, D.C., January 29-31, 1986. The conference made a major contribution to the dialogue about risk by clearly identifying risk communication as an important subject in its own right. It also was by far the largest and most important gathering of risk communication scholars that has been held. For many of the 500 attendees, it was the first realization of the number and variety of other individuals who were studying communications about risk. The conference background paper (reprinted here as an appendix) was the first authoritative compilation and synthesis of the risk communication literature.

Although the conference transcript has been severely edited, we have not tried to rewrite the papers to make them scholarly articles. Rather, consistent with the focus of a conference on communication, we have tried to preserve the spirit of interchange and informality that prevailed.

The conference was the brainchild of Vincent T. Covello of the National Science Foundation and Frederick W. Allen of the U.S. Environmental Protection Agency. They not only formulated the basic purposes and content of the conference but also continued to guide the execution of the plans throughout. At an early stage, they enlisted the assistance of J. Clarence (Terry) Davies, executive vice-president of The Conservation Foundation, and he and the Foundation took responsibility for the details of the conference and for publishing the proceedings.

The conference was cosponsored by The Conservation Foundation, the National Science Foundation, the U.S. Environmental Protection Agency, the University of Southern California, the American Industrial Health Council (AIHC), and the following individual AIHC members: Monsanto Company, American Petroleum Institute, Shell Oil Company, Dow Chemical Company, and Procter and Gamble Company. Dr. Fred Hoerger was particularly helpful in organizing the AIHC support.

Support for preparing the proceedings for publication has been provided by the Environmental Protection Agency and the National Science Foundation. Martha S. Cooley did an excellent job of editing a difficult manuscript. Pam Herring devoted many hours ably transcribing tapes to produce the first version of the manuscript. Gwen Harley retyped a number of subsequent versions with her usual patience and good cheer.

William K. Reilly
President
The Conservation Foundation

Introduction

J. Clarence Davies
Executive Vice-President, The Conservation Foundation

On behalf of the organizers of the conference, I would like to describe briefly the purposes that we hope the conference will serve.

Our first purpose is to recognize risk communication as a field of study and activity that is worthy of recognition in its own right. Some of you have known that for a long time, but I have been impressed at how seldom risk communication is recognized as a separate area. This came home to me quite vividly when I was making phone calls asking people to be on the program for this conference. I talked to several people who, in effect, make their living as risk communicators. That is what they do all day long, but when I asked them to come talk about risk communication they said, "Gee, I don't know much about that." It is a bit like the Moliére character who discovers he has been speaking prose all these years. There has not, until very recently at least, been widespread recognition of risk communication as an important subject.

One corollary of this is that the conference has been designed specifically to focus on the risk communication process. The agenda does not cover risk assessment issues such as the relative importance of different risks or the degree of risk in any particular activity. If we begin talking about that, then we are doing the wrong thing and will be off on a different subject. It is obviously a related subject, and we can't ignore it; but what we want to focus on here is the process of

1

trying to communicate risks, not the evaluation of risks.

Our premise is that the risk communication process is very often unsatisfactory for everybody involved. Those who send messages often feel that their messages have not been received, and the recipients often feel that their questions have not been answered. In short, both miscommunication and noncommunication occur in the risk communication process.

Given this fact, the conference has two further purposes that are absolutely central. One is to identify what is right and what is wrong with the way we currently communicate information about risk; the second is to suggest ways in which the risk communication process can be improved. The program has been structured to address these questions. I am not under any illusion that we will have definitive answers at the end of the conference, but we hope we will have made some progress.

Overviews of the Problem
Communicating about Risk

William D. Ruckelshaus
Former Administrator, U.S. Environmental Protection Agency (EPA)

In the next day and a half, all of us will address an important piece of the puzzle of how our society manages risk—namely, how we communicate the nature of risks to the general public that the government is supposed to protect. When I say "we," I do mean the government, which is charged with the responsibility of managing risk. Having twice been the administrator of the EPA, I still find it difficult not to say "we" when thinking of regulators. Maybe after my third term I will get over that.

During this conference you will examine the various elements and complexities of risk communication, starting with how people perceive risk. We have learned that it is crucial to start with the raw material in this case, public attitudes toward what we are talking about. If we don't start with an understanding of the view of the receptor, we are doomed to failure. You will be discussing the impact on public attitudes of controllable versus uncontrollable risks, voluntary versus involuntary risks, micro versus macro risks—the macro risk being what the EPA administrator says the risk is, the micro risk being what the American people think it is. Often they are not close to being the same thing. You will discuss the concepts of dreaded and unknown risks versus comfortable and known risks. You will discuss how we create and maintain trusted institutions and credible spokespeople. All these questions

3

are crucial. You will look at case studies involving natural risks such as cholesterol and salt and man-induced risks such as ethylene dibromide. On your agenda are nuclear power and hazardous waste sites. By the time this conference is over, you will have run the gamut of the kinds of problems that we have been trying to communicate to people for the last several decades.

Let me talk a bit about why we are worried about communication about risk. What difference does it make? Why don't we simply make decisions involving nuclear power or cancer-causing chemicals, announce them, and get on with it? Why do we even try to involve the public in terrible problems that they have so much difficulty wrestling with? Well, as all of us know, the option of silence is long gone. The reason it has gone, and I think it is important to occasionally reflect back on this, stems from a profound public reaction, first to the Vietnam War and then to Watergate. The public response to these two national traumas was to take back power that had been delegated to the government. Ours is a government of the people in this country, and it derives, as we have been told since we were children, its just powers from the consent of the governed. If the governed withhold that consent or take a portion of it back, it simply means that the government has been forced to once again share the power to govern with those who had earlier given their consent.

In the foreign policy area, power was taken back when Congress began to insist, during the Vietnam era, on having a larger role in dictating the actual conduct of our foreign policy. We have seen several recent manifestations of this insistence. Two freshmen senators went to Nicaragua on the eve of a Senate vote on support for the Administration's request for aid to the Contras. These senators negotiated directly with the president of that country and then returned and told their colleagues in the Senate what the situation was like. We also have seen senators standing in back of our three arms-control negotiators in Geneva as they started the disarmament talks again, in order to ensure that the Senate had a proper presence at this delicate stage of international negotiations. Presumably the senators reported back to their colleagues that everything seemed to be working out all right. And we have seen, just in the last few days, a senator and a team going to observe an election in the Philippines. It seems that there has been some shifting of power, since the Reagan-Gorbachev summit, toward more executive-branch autonomy; but still, there has been a take-back of power by Congress, in terms of foreign policy, which is probably unprecedented in our history.

The Watergate scandal eroded the necessary public trust in the government, and again there was a take-back of power. The form it took on the domestic side and as it relates to regulation of health, safety, and the environment was a demand by the public, via Congress, for a piece of the action, for a right to be involved in the decision-making process. Congress, as it almost always does in response to such demands, acted. It acted by passing laws such as the Freedom of Information Act. All our environmental laws grant several rights to citizens to intervene in the administrative process, to demand hearings. Written into the laws are often very stringent deadlines, along with citizens' rights to go to court and contest the failure of the regulatory agencies to act—that is, rights of participation. At the state level, right-to-know laws are moving very rapidly through state legislatures and are probably going to find their way into laws such as Superfund, if it is ever reauthorized, and others. Probably the only way that those provisions won't be in the laws is if the laws themselves are not reauthorized, which, of course, is fairly probable with many of them. Again, however, this is simply part of the same phenomenon of a take-back of power.

My point here is not to say whether a sharing of the power to make risk management decisions is right or wrong; it is simply to state that it is a fact of life in the United States. We have decided, in an unprecedented way, that the decision-making responsibility involving risk issues must be shared with the American people, and we are very unlikely to back away from that decision. So the question before us is not whether there is going to be a sharing, whether we will have participatory democracy with regard to the management of risk, but how. How do we make decisions effectively, efficiently, and in a timely way, keeping the quality of the decisions high and at the same time involving the public?

Now, none of this will work unless we figure out how we are going to effectively involve the public. There are a couple of principles that we need to bear in mind, at least two of which, certainly one, have a direct bearing on the purpose of this conference. Certain elements need to be present for participatory democracy or public involvement to work. The first is access to the decision maker. That is relatively simple: it is usually guaranteed by statute that the citizen has the right to participate in the decision-making process by testifying at hearings, submitting written testimony, and having access to documents that underlie the decision itself. There is in this whole process an almost unprecedented openness, at least in the historic sense.

The second principle, which is important and particularly relevant to this conference, is that before access can become meaningful, there must be sufficient information in the hands of the public for citizens to be effective participants. The process of supplying this information is at the heart of risk communication. If citizens are going to be effective, they simply have to have sufficient information, not all the information that the decision maker has, but enough so that they can be wrestling with the same kinds of problems and can therefore be useful participants in the whole process.

The information that is provided by the decision maker has to be honest, clear, and as complete as we know how to make it. It does seem that one thing that needs to be focused on, as a crucial aspect of governmental risk communication, is placing a high premium on honesty. If we don't know something, we must say we don't know, and if we are uncertain, we must say we are uncertain. And I don't care whether we are informing people before the decision or whether we are trying to sell the decision after we make it. Where risk communication usually starts to break down, insofar as honesty is concerned, is after the decision is made and there is a perceived necessity to sell a very uncertain, shaky judgment to the American people. Unless we inculcate very deeply in our risk management agencies a real and perceived honesty in communication, we are going to lose the opportunity to bring the public along in understanding and in responding sensibly to the mix of issues that need to be weighed.

Now, I could get into the Tacoma Smelter.* That one is going to be pawed over so much that no one is going to be able to recognize it after we're finished. This incident involved a direct effort by EPA to communicate. Fortunately, we had all the elements of public participation there; the public was aware of both the economic and the environmental impacts of the potential decision. Therefore, I think we

---

*Editor's note: When faced with the decision as to what arsenic air pollution standard to impose on an ASARCO smelter in Tacoma, Washington, Ruckelshaus made an unprecedented effort to involve the community in the decision-making process.

had a better chance of getting the public effectively involved. And we tried all kinds of things: we tried workshops, we tried the media. We were asking the media to participate in providing information as straightforwardly and honestly as they could, and they were, in fact, very helpful. We approached them saying, "You are the vehicle by which most people are going to receive this information, and it is terribly important that it be as accurate as we know how to make it." The media were really very cooperative, not on the editorial page but in the news stories, in trying to present information as accurately as possible.

We could move from there to a kind of macro-communication problem involved in ethylene dibromide (EDB) and how that affected people. I will share with you one anecdote about the media with EDB. This was one of those issues in which we had close to a national panic involving the cancer-causing potential of this grain and citrus fumigant, the residues of which were showing up in food. We wrestled with how to handle the issue for several months. The morning on which I was going to announce the EPA's decision, being a little bit sleepless, I got up early and turned on a television program. There was Charlie Rose, who is on from two to five in the morning. He is a straightforward, balanced, intelligent man. He said, "Now we're going to be faced today with a very important problem. The government is about to make a decision on EDB, a grain fumigant. And fortunately we have two experts who are going to tell us about this decision and what the government's action is likely to be." He then described how the pesticide was used to keep the fruit flies off citrus and keep bugs out of grain. "We have Dr. Epstein in Illinois, who will tell us his views, and then we have Dr. Haverner, an industry representative." Rose first said, "Now, Dr. Epstein, what do you think about this problem?" Dr. Epstein said, "Well, the real problem is not grain or citrus, it's gasoline. Ninety-five percent of EDB is used in gasoline, and as we pump this into our cars it's floating around in the atmosphere and Lord knows what's happening to us." Rose said, "Gasoline? I thought it was grain." "No," Dr. Epstein responded, "it's gasoline, and that's the problem." Rose said, "Well, all right. Dr. Haverner, what do you think?" Dr. Haverner said, "Well, now look, the aflotoxin in peanut butter is 20 times as carcinogenic as EDB is on any human being. We ought to be worried about that." And Charlie Rose said, "Peanut butter?" Then turned to the camera and said, "Gasoline?" He continued, "You can see this is a very complicated subject."

That was when I knew I was home free. There was no way I could confuse people more than that program did. I felt perfectly confident when going into that press conference.

There must be choices confronting the public if we are going to ask them to participate in a meaningful way. The public must have the opportunity to make the real choices that our society faces. Again, in the case of Tacoma, the public had the whole equation. We had an opportunity to engage in a risk communication process that had a chance of working. And in a sort of gross sense it did work in Tacoma: the public did, after a lot of wrenching, come to grips with the real social issues, the same ones that the decision maker has to wrestle with. Unless we have a system that forces the public, which has demanded to become involved, to confront the real choices, then we have a flawed system.

Unfortunately, in the case of Superfund, where people who are living around the toxic sites and who have demanded and been given the right to participate in deciding how to deal with these sites, are asked, "What level of risk would you like to see reduced?" the public is being given only half the equation. Its answer, a very logical one for the individuals involved, is: "I'd like to see all of the risk reduced. I would not like to face any of the risk myself." But the social question is what level of risk should be reduced and at what cost. We can essentially, not in every case but essentially, eliminate risks if we are willing to spend enough. But, given the current budget debates in Congress, it's unlikely that the money will be there; thus, the decision maker is left with a process that is underfunded and a public that is by right involved, but given only half the equation.

In short, the bottom line is forcing the public to be responsive to the real issues. The public must then ultimately take the responsibility for the decision that is finally made. The public can't have it both ways. Citizens can't come in and then get out when they want to; they can't participate in the part of the decision making that's straightforward and stay out of the part that's tough or that might make a neighbor angry or cause some inconvenience or some perceived or real inequity. Accepting responsibility for the final decision is the duty of citizenship. If there is a demand to get involved, then people should get involved; but if they are not involved the whole way, then participatory democracy is not working.

The truth is that we are in the very early stages of trying this, moving from the "whether" to the "how" part of talking about these problems with the public. How do we do it honestly, straightforwardly? Our task is to elicit from people a response that is both sensible and consistent with their own interests. Whether we can be successful in doing this is an open question. Many of my colleagues at EPA, along with the rest of the developed world, think we're mad to try this. Some countries are angry at us because they are certain they are going to be dragged in behind us and will have to wrestle with their publics as we are with ours. I don't believe that either we are mad or they will be, once we begin to understand the elements of success and have successfully experienced involving the public in such judgments. If our democracy is going to work, and if we are going to continue to prosper, we *have* to raise public understanding far beyond where it is now.

I don't believe that technology is our master or that it is going to master us. We are a smart enough people to take advantage of the fruits of technological advances and to minimize or eliminate risks to people and the environment. We can learn from our mistakes. If the lessons we learn from what happened yesterday don't cause us to lose our self-confidence and our sense of wonder today, we will be all right, and so will our country.

Science and Risk Communication

Frank Press
President, National Academy of Sciences (NAS)

As we begin the conference on risk communication, some of you may be noting certain possible dangers set before you. You may be reminding yourselves of Richard Wilson's account of the daily risks we all face. Thus, in coming down to breakfast, Wilson—a Harvard physicist— recalls that 16,000 people die every year from falls. In sweetening his coffee, he wonders whether to use sugar and risk heart disease, or to take saccharin and risk cancer. He attends a committee meeting and worries about the cigarette smoke. He takes a glass of water and thinks about the possible presence of chloroform and the associated carcinogenic hazards. At night, he puts on pajamas, but not without worrying about their flammability. And if the pajamas are labeled as nonflammable, he is reminded of Tris.* Finally, in turning out the lights, he remembers that more people die in bed than anywhere else.

Having bowed to Harvard, I cannot resist repeating a story told by a former colleague at MIT, Norman Rasmussen. He was asked to lecture a lot, especially after he introduced fault-tree analysis to a skeptical public. And he would often begin by asking whether anyone in the audience would accept 10 million dollars. There was only one catch: although nothing would happen to any takers immediately, once they

---

*Editor's note: Tris is a chemical that was widely used as a flame-retardant on children's sleepwear before animal tests indicated that it might cause cancer.

left the lecture room there was a one-in-ten chance that they would die on the spot. He asked for volunteers to take the money. No hands were raised. He then lowered the risk to one in a hundred, then to one in a thousand. Still no takers. He made it one in a million. And then a few hands went up. He smiled with delight and pointed out that the risk of an accident in driving three miles to his talk was greater than one in a million. And so, at last, he had met people who really thought it was worth 10 million dollars to hear him talk.

I have been asked to supply a scientific perspective on risk communication. This is a mischievous topic because it implies that science can somehow clear out the fogginess that invariably envelops this issue. Of course, it cannot. Risk communication is a buzzword for a nest of vipers that includes semantics, laws and regulations, potential economic costs, and the shotgun wedding of law and science.

Risk communication is also a mischievous topic because it implies that science is somehow outside the issue itself. But, again, that is not true. As you are quite aware, an uncertainty principle operates in science and the communication of risk. The very act of scientists turning their attention to a given risk changes the public's view of that risk. As Paul Slovic has pointed out, an engineer counting up improbabilities in various branches of a fault-tree analysis does not reassure his audience; he scares it. By listing all the things that could go wrong, the engineer both informs and disturbs.

A further reason why science and risk communication denote a mischievous arena is that, in it, science often becomes transscience. Transscience was defined by Alvin Weinberg as involving questions that can be asked but not answered by science. The reasons for the appearance of transscience in issues of risk analysis are clear: the issues are invariably badly structured. They are often messy. They are posed under enormous pressures of politics, economics, and deadlines. They are rarely, if ever, susceptible to a crisp solution. In this business, we do not have one-armed scientists, nor are we ever likely to.

That said, let me try to be a bit more helpful by suggesting some areas where the role of science in risk communication can indeed be strengthened—both in how that role is played out and in how it is conveyed. My suggestions are framed within a maturing understanding of the realities of risk communication and perception. For example, although we may wonder why it took us so long to arrive at this conclusion, we now accept human nature as a given when we think about risk. We now appreciate that, although generally people may be frightened by the idea of risk, they are remarkably indifferent to some risks and remarkably leery of others.

A colleague of mine tells a story that capsulizes this nicely. After the movie *Jaws* came out, it was not uncommon to see New England beaches emptied after someone spotted what seemed to be a shark but usually turned out to be flotsam. People would rush to their cars and take off at high speed, but few would buckle their seat belts. And no one can remember the last time a shark attacked anyone in New England waters. In light of the statistics of car accidents versus shark bites, the impulse to flee the beach is absurd, but it is also real. Having seen the movie, people could visualize getting bitten by sharks, but no one was willing to admit to being a bad driver. Indeed, in one study it was found that 90 to 95 percent of those asked rated their driving abilities as average or above.

There are more realities of human nature that affect risk communication. People tend to overestimate the incidence of some risks, such as homicides, and to underestimate others, especially diseases such as diabetes. And these beliefs tend to be quite durable. Even when told otherwise, people hold on to certain beliefs. They are supremely confident that what they know is really so. Thus, when people give a-thousand-to-one odds that a particular "fact" is correct, they are actually wrong 10 to 20 percent of the time. That is not an indictment of human nature; it is simply another warning light for our efforts to understand both the perception and the communication of risk.

Finally, in thinking about a role for science in risk communication, we have to acknowledge that different people react quite differently to the same risk. The point is made in telling fashion in William Clark's version of the story of *The Lady or the Tiger*:

> The young man could open either door he pleased. If he opened the one, there came out of it a hungry tiger, the fiercest and most cruel that could be procured, which would immediately tear him to pieces. But if he opened the other door, there came from it a lady, the most suitable to his years and station that His Majesty could select among his fair subjects. So I leave it to you, which door to open?
>
> The first man refused to take the chance. He lived safely and died chaste.
>
> The second man hired risk assessment consultants. He collected all of the available data on lady and tiger populations. He brought in sophisticated technology to listen for growling and to detect the faintest whiff of perfume. He

completed checklists. He developed a utility function and assessed his risk averseness. Finally, sensing that in a few more years he would be in no condition to enjoy the lady anyway, he opened the optimal door. And was eaten by a low-probability tiger.

The third man took a course in tiger taming. He opened a door at random and was eaten by a cannibalistic lady.

This story is not the most promising, for the only survivor is the one who retreated from the risk. Those who armed themselves with knowledge or courage were eaten. As William Clark points out, "the analysis that predicts the tiger will always be surprised by the carnivorous lady." Our ignorance is likely to remain greater than our knowledge.

The easy response is that, although the tiger was unavoidable, matters such as toxic chemicals often are not. The world is interdependent, technically complex, and littered with things that may be harmful and are sometimes unavoidable. The role of science in this world is clear-cut: it must inform the analyses of risks. And it must strive to improve the quality of what it does, its precision and accuracy, its tools, and the soundness of its interpretations.

Yet, although better science is a *sine qua non*, there are limits. Most obviously, there are the limits of incompleteness and uncertainty. In the EDB (ethylene dibromide) episode Mr. Ruckelshaus, as EPA administrator, had to acknowledge, in spite of heroic efforts to understand EDB's potential harm, that the EPA was operating "in an area of enormous scientific uncertainty."

It is important to understand that uncertainties are not unique to matters of risk. They are really what drives all of science. If there were certainty, there would be no science. Science is an endlessly changing series of approximations, whether the issue be the creation of the universe, the shapes of continents, the chemistry of the upper atmosphere, or the effects of a foreign chemical on living cells.

In short, uncertainty is routine in science. In risk analyses, the uncertainty of science butts up against the law's rigid demands for certainty. The law does not have much tolerance for the sort of tentativeness that is understood, respected, even admired, in science. As the British physicist John Ziman once pointed out, "in science, as in law, we are almost always dealing with theories that are disputable, and that can be challenged by an appeal to evidence for or against them." When evidence conflicts, scientists repeat the experiment. That option is generally not available in law, where disputes must be settled with yes or no. The upshot is that the elusiveness of scientific certainty, when highlighted by the yes/no demands of law, translates into a public perception of evasiveness. That is not an admission of failure, but simply an acknowledgment of reality.

Scientists have become ever more sophisticated in operating in this arena of incomplete data, sometimes heroic extrapolations, and the like. They increasingly and responsibly understand the need to reach probable conclusions, even in the absence of complete data. Scientists remain, of course, bemused by political processes: by the glacial pace and sometimes illogical turns of regulatory action, and by the sometimes quirky turns of decision making. These are not unfamiliar patterns.

Consider the history of saccharin, which baited controversy almost from the day it was created in 1878. At the beginning of this century, Harvey Wiley was called an idiot by Theodore Roosevelt for suggesting that saccharin was harmful to health. A committee of the U.S. Department of Agriculture cleared it, but it was banned anyway, apparently to protect the sugar industry. A sugar shortage in World War I put saccharin back on the market. In 1978, a committee of the National Academy of Sciences, in its fifth study, found saccharin to be a weak carcinogen. But Congress passed a special act to keep it on the market.

That is a paradoxical history. When saccharin was declared blameless, it was banned, and when it was found harmful under certain conditions, it was kept on the market by a Congress influenced by a mix of politics, economics, and science.

We can be amused by that history, but it supplies yet another dimension to the new reality I spoke of earlier: the better appreciation of the uses of science. That appreciation has taken hold in the scientific community, which has come to be more sensitive to the pressures dictating public action, even in the face of limited precision as to measurements and observations.

The tentativeness of science, although infuriating at times, can also be a buffer against precipitous actions. We have seen hasty actions lead to high costs and dubious benefits, and delays yield productive compromises. Henry James said of science that it is the "absence of prejudice in the presence of money." That absence of prejudice is indeed what science is about. Science is not looking at tissue slides; it is not instruments sniffing the air or testing the water. Science is about testable conclusions based on often disputable facts. It is about a community of professionals coming to reasonable agreements on matters riddled with uncertainties and incomplete data. It is in that context, underlain by an absence of prejudice, that science has a critical role in both the perception and the communication of risk.

That said, we still have to acknowledge the classic Zen problem of the sound of one hand clapping. Although risks are increasingly being uncovered and appraised, we lag badly in telling people the meaning of this. We lack an adequate language for communicating the conclusions of science, with all the messy uncertainties. Probabilities, error bars, and the like do not work; they invite a certain petulance. I am reminded that a former commissioner of the Food and Drug Administration, on being told that a scientific panel was 95 percent certain that cyclamates do not cause cancer, said that he did not need a "wishy-washy, iffy" answer.

Glib comparisons—say, comparing exposure to asbestos to driving a car—justifiably anger people who understand the difference between involuntary and voluntary risks. And burying the real world in the cryptic language of science invites bafflement. There is a famous story told by the Nobelist Felix Bloch of his studies with Werner Heisenberg. One day, Bloch brightly announced to Heisenberg that space is simply the field of linear operations—to which Heisenberg said: "Nonsense! Space is blue and birds fly through it."

In matters of risk, high-quality science has to be partnered with the language to express it, clearly and accurately. We have to remember that space is blue. But how should we talk to the public in words that are scientifically defensible *and* clear? How do we clarify the miasma of error bars, probabilities, and the like?

The problem is more than simply one of semantics. Often, public pronouncements on risks tend to be put in policy terms. They tend to be in macro rather than micro language. It is macro language that estimates the global likelihood that a given chemical will lead to cancer. The pronouncements are not in micro language that would tell the housewife whether she should buy a cake powder tinged with traces of EDB.

I hope that this conference will consider these matters. How are risks communicated sensibly to the public? And how do we frame those risks at levels important to that housewife or the worker in front of a lathe or a video display terminal? In doing so, we ought to note certain givens.

One is that the public is, by and large, more sophisticated about risks than we give it credit for. Another is that the public truly wants to know about risk, even if the answers are not happy ones. Finally, the qualitative aspects of a risk are usually more important to people than accurate estimates. Equating risks with statistical probabilities is often irrelevant and at times quite distorting.

What, then, do we do? Conferences such as this one are an important step. So are well-organized meetings between scientists and news reporters to articulate the gap between describing a problem carefully and reporting it succinctly. Just such a conference was organized by Georgetown University and held in 1984 at the National Academy of Sciences (NAS). We need to continue such meetings.

The NAS is taking various approaches to improve the communication of scientific issues, including risks. We do so through occasional seminars for special audiences such as congressional staff. We also have an op-ed service, in which carefully reviewed, clearly written analyses of scientific issues are provided to some 100 newspapers. And we intend to do more. For example, the time is ripe for a weekly television program reporting on current developments in science and technology. Such a program would, of course, deal with the sorts of issues now before this conference. These efforts, combined with many others, will help us grope toward a new dialect, a new way of talking about risk. But, so far, the failures in the communication of risk are more apparent than the successes. I hope that this conference can prompt a change.

Why We Must Talk about Risk

Lee M. Thomas
Administrator, U.S. Environmental Protection Agency (EPA)

I have spent most of my time in government in jobs where one of the main things I have had to do is to tell people about the danger they might be in. That's certainly a major part of being a public safety director and of working in the emergency-response field—my former positions. Of course, at the EPA we're trying to make it a central part of the administrator's job.

Nearly everything government does involves some form of risk communication. I would like to take this opportunity to give you my personal view of this complex and troublesome business, to try to put it in a broader context than that of environmental protection. I also want to discuss why risk communication has changed in recent years: why it's tougher than it used to be, why it will probably get tougher yet, and why we can't afford to relent in our efforts to learn how to do it better.

The Constitution tells us to provide for the general welfare, and we have defined that mandate broadly in recent times. In dozens of ways the government tries to stand between people and the risks resulting from natural or man-made phenomena. In the past, governments have approached this task through the use of experts. The expert examined the risk, made a judgment about how much risk was tolerable, and pronounced a particular situation safe or not safe. In these judgments

19

some residual risk was always allowed; the experts knew this, but it wasn't common to talk about it. The government considered that it had done its duty if it had arranged for a reputable person to vouch for the safety of a particular process or thing. Most people were satisfied to rely on experts. Little information was available to the general public in any case, and if something did go wrong, it was convenient to have an individual to blame.

This general approach was considered adequate from the earliest days of federal involvement in the public safety arena, which began with the establishment of the Steamboat Inspection Service, through the later development of safety standards for food, drugs, railways, and aircraft. Most of us would agree that this approach is no longer adequate.

It is inadequate for three reasons. First, the kind of risks we are most concerned about have changed as a direct result of changes in technology. Modern risks such as those discussed here are subtle, hard to quantify, exotic in their origins, and usually involuntarily assumed. Compare, for example, the differences between running the EPA and running the Steamboat Inspection Service. If your steamboat inspection program is working right, the number of explosions should decline over time. This is easy to check; there should be a good correlation between the stringency of your standards and the risk of completing a steamboat voyage unharmed. Obviously, those simple days are gone forever.

The second reason is that the public has changed. The American people are both better informed and less tolerant of risks to life and health. There is ample information available about risks, most of it accessible to the nonexpert. It may not be correct, but it is available. This has tended to diminish expert knowledge in the public eye, as has the often reported spectacle of distinguished experts in violent disagreement. Moreover, for a number of familiar reasons, the public no longer trusts government as much as it once did. In disputes about risk, agents of the government may be seen by the public as pursuing institutional or political interests of their own.

Finally, government itself has changed. It is expected to be more open, more responsive, more forthcoming than ever before, especially at the federal level. Because of that, those of us in government can't simply provide for the general welfare as a benevolent despot would. A British jurist once explained the necessity for open trials by saying, "Not only must justice be done; it must be seen to be done." In the same vein, we must not only protect but also be seen to protect.

For these reasons we can no longer simply establish safety standards through expert judgments arrived at privately. The response of government to a perceived risk must take place within the full view of the public—hence our new emphasis on risk communication.

This is happening throughout government. In one of my former jobs, for example, I had to make presentations to the state legislature on behalf of a program for releasing prisoners into the community. I had to communicate the risk that these people might commit other crimes. Such risks are difficult to determine, yet they elicit strong opposition and debate. In siting prisons and halfway houses you have to explain these same risks to a local community. (Siting prisons is quite similar to siting hazardous waste facilities, by the way: everybody wants the capacity, but nobody wants to live next to the place.) I've also had responsibilities in highway safety and emergency preparedness, and it's the same there as well. The job entails not only buying the maximum level of public safety with limited resources, but also explaining the connection between risk reduction and any imposed inconveniences.

Risk communication has thus become the inevitable responsibility of nearly all areas of government. Having said that, I must add that environmental risk is unusual in several ways that contribute to the difficulty of risk communication in this area.

To begin with, at the EPA we must work with a very broad definition of risk. There are risks to human health, of course, but there are also risks to particular ecological resources, to various measures of welfare, and to the integrity of the environment as a whole. Different policies may have different or even opposite effects on each of these, and we have to explain this to the public.

Research indicates that our difficulty in dealing with a particular risk is a function of how familiar it is and of how dreaded its final effect. Many environmental risks score low in the first and high in the second category. The chemical compounds that pose risks are often exotic, with strange, alphabet-soup names. They are suspected of causing cancer and birth defects. We fear cancer in a way that we don't fear car crashes, which is one reason why many Americans are extremely sensitive to risks arising from environmental contaminants.

Another factor is the inability of science to produce definitive answers to questions about environmental risk. If we know our degree of risk, we can get used to it, even if it is quite high. Indeterminate risks, however, can breed infinite fear.

But I think the greatest difficulty lies in our inability to confront the phenomenon of residual risk and deal with it in a constructive way. By "residual risk" I mean that risk that remains after society has expended all the resources it can afford for purposes of control. We may argue about what we can afford, but as any society's resources are in the end finite, some residual risk must inevitably exist. This has become more obvious with our increased ability to detect ever smaller concentrations of pollutants. It is also in the nature of things that some places are riskier to live than other places and that some individuals bear more risk than others. The latter may complain that, while society at large gains the benefits of a technology that produces pollution, society does not bear the risks—they do.

It is hard for a society such as ours, publicly dedicated to equality and valuing so highly life and health, to confront this reality. Our discomfort has made it politically advantageous to foster the illusion of infinite resources. The EPA is often called on, for example, to eliminate all risk at a particular place, with the implied assumption that "somebody else" will pay for it. The situation is complicated by the way that we partition risks into "voluntary" and "involuntary" categories. We have evidence that smoking is perhaps the major controllable public health problem in the country. We don't ban smoking; smoking is a voluntary risk. So is driving, but drivers kill thousands of "involuntary" pedestrians. We accept that, too; people who walk on public thoroughfares in a society dominated by private transportation are expected to submit to a certain risk. So it is odd that risks associated with the production of materials and energy, functions that are vital to our way of life, are totally rejected as "involuntary" and intolerable at vanishingly low levels.

Such is the emotional arena in which risk communication must take place. We have our work cut out for us. Perhaps communication is, after all, too modest a concept. What I think we have to do is to re-educate ourselves with respect to risk, so that as a society we can make sensible public judgments about safety.

This will take some time, and it will expose those who attempt it to political risks. Residual environmental risk is plain bad news. Why spread this news? We must if we intend to serve the broadest public interest. To do so, we have to accept and publicize the reality that our society generates risk in the course of making a living for everyone in it. But when you defend the broad public interest, there tend to be ranged against you certain special interests: the "not-in-my-backyard" interests, the "why-does-it-have-to-be-me" interests, and, of course, the interests of those who bear some responsibility for producing risks in the first place.

Even a cursory study of American politics suggests that, when the general interest and special interests are in conflict, you are wise to back the special interests. Some people believe that bucking special interests is impossible. I used to believe that myself, but now I am convinced that the EPA must take the harder road. Let me turn to some of the practical steps we are taking in that direction.

First, we will continue to express control actions in quantitative risk terms, whenever possible. We will openly discuss the alternatives we have considered in those terms and openly confront the issue of residual risks. For example, we recently promulgated a regulation banning most uses of asbestos. In our announcement, the risks of all the alternatives we considered were clearly indicated, together with their costs. We will also attempt to put environmental risks in a broader context. I want people to understand that risks vary widely in their seriousness, and that the EPA's program is concentrated on the worst ones. I want the EPA to be aggressive in pursuit of risks; when people learn about risk, I want us to break the news in an authoritative and comprehensive way.

Next, we are attempting to increase the consistency and clarity of our scientific base. We are in the process of reviewing the quantitative information on chemical toxicity developed over the years in different parts of the agency, to insure that it is correct and that the agency gives a single answer to questions about each substance we have studied. In the near future we will make efforts to increase direct public access to this store of information.

On the national level we will build risk communication into regulatory policy whenever possible. The Superfund community relations policy is a good example of this approach. In brief, we intend to develop a community relations plan for every Superfund response action lasting longer than five days. For remedial sites these plans must be prepared before remedial investigation work begins. The plans will be based on interviews with state and local officials, civic and community organizations, interested residents, and media representatives.

The most important thing about this program is that it is designed to be a two-way system of communication. We are not going to go into a community and tell people what we intend to do. We are going to listen to local concerns and ideas. It is true that many of the issues involved in a site cleanup are highly technical, but we can no longer use that as an excuse for discounting what a community has to say about risk. We must empower the community to discuss risk in a rational and technically competent way.

We intend to develop a similar community relations program in connection with the permitting of hazardous waste treatment, storage, and disposal facilities under the 1984 RCRA amendments. The pattern of waste disposal is going to change in response to those amendments. Wastes that went into landfills will have to go somewhere else. There will be renewed attention paid to recycling and incineration. We intend to involve the public in the permitting process in the same way that we are involving it in cleanup planning and execution.

It is an odd fact that communities that would not object to, or would even welcome, a manufacturer of chemicals locating nearby will offer strong resistance to a recycling plant or an incinerator if the fatal words "hazardous waste" are used. It is clear that we cannot afford public ignorance in areas where waste disposal facilities are required. The extraordinary difficulties we now have in siting hazardous waste facilities of any kind tells us we need to do a better job.

Not only must we raise, by direct action, the level of sophistication of the public's thinking about risk issues, but we must also do what we can to increase the number of people who can communicate effectively about risk. State and local leaders must become more familiar with the language and skills of risk analysis. We have launched a series of risk assessment workshops for such officials and for our own regional staffs. At these meetings, we take the participants through a model risk assessment to give them a feel for the kind of information that we can derive from scientific inquiry, for the role that judgment must play in the attribution of risk, and for the degree of uncertainty involved.

We are also working with a number of states on pilot projects designed to help them assess environmental risks on a statewide basis and to then set priorities for control. Risk communication is a central part of these projects. Their ultimate goal is to increase public cognizance of the fact that priorities must be set if any real progress is to be made in dealing with environmental risks, and to gain public acceptance of an ordered and rational program to control the most significant risks first.

The coming year will challenge to the utmost our ability to communicate about risk. We will be making extent-of-remedy decisions on at least 50 sites on the Superfund National Priorities List. If we don't learn how to work with the communities involved—if they don't come to feel that the EPA and the state agency and the community are on the same side, grappling with difficult technical and moral problems in the best way we can—then that program is not going to work.

As we move further along and begin addressing different kinds of risks, the need for risk communication will grow. We have been accumulating evidence that in many places the major sources of health risk are not industrial plants or even hazardous waste facilities. They come from things like radon, a natural radioactive product of certain types of rock, from the air in homes, from wood stoves, from gas stations and dry cleaners. Controlling these risks has the potential for seriously affecting individual lives and causing significant personal financial loss. People are not going to go along with programs that have such a potential unless they truly understand the risk they are exposed to and unless they participate fully in decisions about controlling it.

This future will make risk communication more necessary but no easier. The risk communicator has few friends.

But as uncomfortable as it may be, we have no real choices in the matter. Risk communication of the type I have outlined appears to be the only approach that protects the environment while supporting both the democratic and the economic goals of our technological society. We will never return to the days when we were content to let people in white coats make soothing noises. Citizens must share directly in decisions that affect them, and we must ensure that they do so with a fuller understanding of the inevitable trade-offs involved in the management of risk.

Panel

Responsibilities of
Risk Communicators

Alvin Alm, Chairperson
*Former Deputy Administrator, U.S. Environmental Protection Agency
(EPA)*

This panel has representatives from all the major parties in the risk communication process. It will explore what the responsibilities of the media,
industry, environmental groups, and the government are when communicating about risk. Each of these groups has at times been critical
of the others, but there is a widespread recognition that each bears some
responsibility for insuring that the risk communication process is reliable
and responsive.

Tom Vacor
Consumer Reporter, KCBS-Los Angeles

News is what we, the news media, say it is, pure and simple. This gives
us tremendous influence and tremendous power. Where does that power
come from? It comes from the First Amendment to the Constitution,
to be sure. The framers of the Constitution had had an illegal press—
the revolutionary press. If you used it, you went to jail or you were
hung or shot by the king's soldiers. The United States made very sure
in the First Amendment that one of the things that jelled the republic—
freedom of the press—would be protected. That gives us considerable

influence and authority.

As a more practical consideration, either the media transmit the news or you don't receive it. That gives us a technical leg up. But people must invite us into their homes. It does not really matter too much that we own the transmitter, if people are not turning on their TV sets, or the radios, or buying newspapers.

There is a fundamental sense in the United States that what the media do is necessary, although sometimes we do it very badly. And there is the belief that justice is served by a free press—that what we do is an attempt to get at the truth, to promote a better public understanding. Again, sometimes we do not do this very well.

Justice has many possible definitions. Justice, as defined by Webster's Dictionary, is "conformity to moral principles or law." That definition at least implies that there are going to be some rules defined by somebody that we are going to conform to. In a criminal court, however, justice is different. It is bound up in the concept of reasonable doubt. If, as a prosecutor, I cannot prove beyond a reasonable doubt that you are guilty, then you are not guilty, and that is justice. In a civil court, justice is a function of the preponderance of evidence—my evidence on this side, your evidence on that side; whichever weighs a little more wins, and that is justice.

The justice I would like to speak about here is the concept of "media justice," which may be called instant justice. A man is accused of molesting children; we report it. What are the consequences? What if he is innocent? What if he is never prosecuted? What if he is prosecuted but acquitted? Where is the justice?

Another man is the employee of a chemical firm. He leaks information to us, which we are very likely to report, to the effect that his company is polluting the Chesapeake Bay. Because we don't want to have that happening, we go on the air and we report it. But what if this information is only partially true? What if it is true that his company is putting a chemical into the Bay, but the major source of the problem is the firm next door? What are the consequences for his company, the employees, the public? Where is the justice?

The state of Florida bans food with as little as one part per billion of EDB, and the media goes into a frenzy for three months, saying that if you eat muffins you are going to die of cancer. That is in effect what happened. What happens when we find out the insignificance of the dose rate, that the dose rate has been consistent in this population for 40 years with no real evidence of any harm to the population? But the media destroys the only viable, economical way of treating milling machinery for insect infestation. The alternatives are not nearly as good or as palatable, particularly if you consider such things as the irradiation of food.

The point of all this is that most of the information on risk assessment is funneled through the media—local news sources more than national ones. The national news has a half-hour every night to tell you everything of consequence that happened on earth. Risk assessment is very rarely part of that. The nightly national news broadcast is usually a recap of the hits, runs, and errors of the day.

Most local reporters have little or no knowledge of or background in technical matters. Yet when something happens, they are sent out on a story. In 90 minutes or so they must become instant experts because they have got to make the air that night or the deadline for the newspaper. Most of them tend to parrot things that are told to them. Very little local news is analytical, and when it is, it tends to be analytical in the sense of "this is what one side says, this is what the other side says." As I said, we are required to be instant experts, but we rarely investigate further the story of the day. There are big incidents, but there is very little follow-up.

The media's posture with regard to risk is primarily reactive, which is to say that we tend to come in after an incident involving risk. We look primarily for victims: victims make good television, good print. We also investigate the aftermath of incidents, assisted by critics. We like critics because they can look at some event and say that if something had happened or had not happened, there would clearly have been a different outcome. Rarely do we take time to look in advance at things that might happen.

We also often look for officials, for two reasons. First, they are people in authority, although they are in fact rarely authorities. Indeed, they are rarely capable of even commenting on risk issues because of their sensitive news nature. Second, we look for officials because we want to affix blame. If we need someone to blame, we usually choose an official; he or she can be portrayed as asleep at the switch, so to speak.

After interviewing officials, we do a thing called Man on the Street— "What do you think about that?" We go out and get three or four interviews, 10 or 15 seconds from one person or another, and that is the local news.

Now if that sounds critical, it is meant to be. We are reactive, and we are allowed to be that way. You have allowed us to go off half-cocked on a variety of issues. You have not corrected us; you have not given us advance information. The result is exactly what you see in the news media today. What you see is reaction rather than analysis. When you do see analysis, it is not very good analysis. The media are highly speculative. For instance, the media are now trying to figure out what happened to the *Challenger* before any of the experts have collected its parts.* That is what the public demands from us. We are always trying to fix blame.

The reality of the situation is that most viewing or reading audiences are not very attentive. They do not pay much attention to what the media are saying. We are generally background noise for dinner. We are required not to be terribly lengthy in our comments because we tend to bore people.

Why is that important? It is important because it encourages us to look for the smoking government, the body count, or the rocket's red glare. You have seen it all a hundred times, and you will see it a hundred times again. Therefore, you have to educate the media; you have a responsibility to become a participant. If you let us keep going the way we are going, everybody is going to survive, but things are going to become more difficult as our society becomes more technological.

You have to understand the risk that you are communicating, but, more importantly, you have to understand the media. You have to talk to us in advance. You have to involve the public early. If we do not pick up on your information often enough, then you have a legitimate basis for a complaint.

Furthermore, you have to speak to us in English. What is 10 to the minus seventh? What is one part per billion? I may not understand the concept of a billion, but when you explain that one part per billion is one second out of 32 years, that does not seem to be much dosage or much time to be exposed to something that is considered to be so awfully dangerous. There are a lot of extremely dangerous things you can be

---

*Editor's note: This conference was held in late January 1986, a few days after the space shuttle *Challenger* had exploded after take-off.

exposed to for one second out of 32 years and not suffer any great consequences.

So, as scientists, regulators, and policy makers, you have to figure out what the media do, how they work, and how to make them work for you. You have to participate. That means that you must be aggressive rather than reactive. You must help people understand things rather than defending a company or an agency from criticism. You have to learn to deal with media inquiry, to supply information in advance and consider the medium. If you are dealing with television, you do not want to have a group of people sitting up here talking. You want to be able to show pictures. If you are dealing with radio and print, you need to paint pictures with words.

You have to learn how to be a source of information that is trusted. You have to decide who should talk to the media. Very often the media contact is a public relations person who either does not understand the issue or is allowed to speak only the party line. When something bad happens, the person who made the decision should take the heat because the heat will go away that much more quickly. It is crucial to understand how the system works. You have to know how the media format a newscast, a newspaper, or broadcast. You have to understand who the players are, on the screen, on the air, in print, and even more importantly, behind the scenes. You have to understand how to gain access to the nonnews media out there: the feature editors of the newspapers, the morning television shows that you would never think anyone would be interested in, although they have vast audiences and 8 or 10 minutes of unedited time that is almost never utilized. There are great media wastelands that you are not taking advantage of: the weekends, for example. In most major cities, the most watched newscasts are on Sunday evening.

Finally, you have to understand that if you have a news event planned on certain days or when certain types of events occur, you must cancel it. The situation with the *Challenger* is a case in point: if you have a conference or press briefing planned for this week, you should reschedule it, because it is unlikely to be covered.

If you understand how the media work and demand a higher degree of participation in the system, everything will improve. Then, if you see a pattern of abuse, you have a duty to make complaints that may attack the broadcasting license that is damaging your industry or your profession.

Ellen Silbergeld
Senior Scientist, Environmental Defense Fund

I am not sure how I feel about this well-attended conference, because to a certain extent I look upon the subject that we are here to talk about as a result of the destruction of consensus on environmental and other risk areas, which has occurred over the last decade in this country. In fact, I would describe the topic as a shield for inaction. We say that we cannot do anything in the area of determining and managing risk because we do not communicate. I would suggest that we cannot communicate because we do not do anything about managing risk. I would further suggest that there are some real and some false issues that we are talking about here today. The false issues relate to what I see as attempting to market unacceptable risk.

An entire form of miscommunication—almost an art form—is developing which pervades all segments of society. And what has alarmed me in the context of this conference is a suggestion that it is the recipient of information who somehow is to blame for problems in communication. I fear that it is all too easy to wind up blaming the victim once again.

There are nevertheless real issues related to this subject—which I hope is fundamentally managing risk, not talking about it—and they may perhaps fall into three areas. There are issues of content, issues of trust, and very important issues of power that we hardly ever talk about.

I think that we tend to spend a great deal of our time in the area of content, not always very fruitfully. We argue and discuss the manner of presentation, how we are going to handle what we consider to be extremely technical and abstruse information in a way that recipients can understand. I was struck by Judge Jack B. Weinstein's remarks as he concluded the settlement of the Agent Orange product liability litigation [in 1984], in which he said that he had never found juries in Brooklyn to have any problem understanding probability because they spend a lot of time at the race track. Perhaps what we think are great hurdles to understanding are primarily in our minds, not in the minds of the public.

Clearly, there are very important questions related to communicating technical issues. In fact, it is impossible to communicate anything unless we who are doing the communicating or who are responsible for acting have resolved those questions and reached a consensus. But many of the problems in communication that have developed over the last five years have been a result of a determination to not reach consensus, particularly in the environmental area.

Of course, there are real issues that are technical; they relate chiefly to the handling of the uncertainty, both in its scientific dimensions and in terms of how we intend to act in the face of its inevitability. We will never have a situation in which all the technical questions are resolved, either those surrounding theoretical modeling in the area of carcinogen risk assessment or those surrounding the development of a scientific interpretation of ever-increasing amounts of fat in our diet.

The issues of trust in risk communication, which will be dealt with by the next panel, cannot be overemphasized. Communication is stifled primarily when those who are communicating are no longer trusted. There are many reasons why trust is lost. One of the main reasons for the loss of trust is a failure to understand that risk and benefit are not coexistent in our society. That is, we frequently ask people to take on risks of whatever dimensions, quite small or very large, without considering whether they are also going to reap any benefits from the assumption of the risks.

We indulge frequently in risk relativism, and the often-cited table by Dick Wilson and colleagues at Harvard is perhaps the most glaring example of risk relativism. * If there is anyone in this room who cannot understand why that table enrages the public, you need to know a great deal about commonsense psychology, not this new field of risk communication.

Trust has also been lessened to a great extent because the public has seen that often what is being discussed are rationales for inaction, not rationales for action. We are much more often discussing what I would call excuses for not acting rather than reasons for performing actions at a particular level or on a particular timetable.

And finally those who develop information on risk have indulged in exploitation of those who do not have this information. I would like to briefly touch on the issue of power, because it is intimately involved in any setting where one party is communicating something to another. Power can be wielded, in the area of environmental politics as in any

---

*Editor's note: The table lists a variety of disparate causes, all of which result in the same amount of risk.

other area, only when there are opportunities for choice on all sides. All the interested parties must be included, and they must have some opportunity to choose from a menu of various options, risk assessments, or other kinds of judgments and decisions to be made.

Power also entails a distribution of equity. This goes back to the question of risks and benefits, and our failure to understand that people come to the table from different equity positions. One of the important issues of equity, which has struck me strongly with regard to risk communication, is equal access to technical information. Equal access to resources is needed to understand the issues, to go behind the presentation being made by the communicator—to reassess the risks, if you will, to reevaluate the grounds for decisions and discussions.

In our society, we deal with the unequal distribution of power primarily by providing options for negotiation. We should consider the work of this conference, and the work of risk communication, to be an exercise in risk negotiation. How can we better negotiate among all parties in our society with respect to disseminating information on risk and setting agendas for dealing with it?

In any negotiation, all parties involved must be present. The fundamental as well as the specific issues at hand must be on the table and open for discussion. It is not possible for communicators of risk assessment information to continue to discuss technical details without coming to grips with real concerns that the scientific and other communities have about the theoretical and practical bases of risk assessment. We can no longer avoid that issue.

We must consider action and inaction as options of equal value. If we are always presenting the option of relative inaction, of not doing something, of delaying something, of balancing things, then we are not really negotiating.

I hope that from this conference we will come to some useful understanding of the real issues. We must not continue to blame the victims, the recipients of information, or to believe that we cannot do anything because we can no longer communicate—when the reverse may be true.

Etcyl H. Blair
*Vice-President and Director of Health and Environmental Sciences, Dow
Chemical Company* *

As a scientist and a manager in the chemical industry, I have a responsibility to see that potentially hazardous situations are identified and
that both data and insights are developed so that my company, its
employees, its customers, and various publics can use this information
to avoid harm. I strongly believe that risk information should be fac-
tually correct and provide some perspective that is useful.

As a businessman and risk manager, my communications must be
tailored to meet the needs of various audiences, including employees.
Within a corporation the size of Dow Chemical, tens of thousands of
scientists and engineers are communicating along various lines about
risk assessment and hazards. In addition, we must communicate with
government officials, transportation officials, customers, and a variety of others. We also need to communicate with the media and those
who are involved in long-term educational and research endeavors. Although we have tens of thousands of chemists and chemical engineers,
we probably have only a couple dozen news media people.

Sometimes I initiate communications; at other times I merely respond
to outside inquiries on such issues as new findings on potentially adverse
health effects of our products (for example, an increased risk of cancer
and birth defects). Some of these findings originate in our research
laboratories.

We also have to consider crisis communication, such as communication of transportation accidents and chemical spills. Moreover, we have
to deal with questions from government officials, regulators, and courts
who sometimes ask for our opinion on events in which we are not even
involved. So, we deal with many audiences.

The American Society of Newspaper Editors says, in its statement
of principles, that "the primary purpose of gathering and distributing
news and opinion is to serve the general welfare by informing the people and enabling them to make judgments on the issues of the time."
I would like to think that we could define the purpose of risk communication in a similar manner: "to serve the general welfare by providing

---

*Mr. Blair left Dow Chemical Company in 1986.

people with the information they need to make knowledgeable judgments on risk." It is the responsibility of the risk communicator first to understand the risk and then to communicate it in such a way that the audience can make an informed decision on how to respond. In other words, it is not simply enough to yell fire.

Unfortunately, several things get in the way of effective risk communication. Industry faces three specific problems. First, it is extremely difficult to distinguish between low and high risks. Mr. Ruckelshaus has underscored the need to communicate meaningfully about the gradients of risk. This is difficult for industry because the warning signals—cancer, birth defects, dangers to unborn children, the so-called time bombs—are already implanted in the public's mind. Adversarial approaches to rule making and litigation, even with the most objective of reporting, keep public debate alive for years as the problem is being considered.

One might ask how a particular risk compares to other risks and to what extent that risk can be reduced. It is certainly worthwhile to see to what extent it is practical to do so, and at what cost to society. For society ultimately bears the final cost in all these determinations.

A number of examples of these questions exist today—emissions of small quantities of toxic air pollutants; parts per billion of carcinogens in water; small amounts of natural carcinogens in our foods or elsewhere; our technological ability to detect even minute quantities of toxins. Our information-gathering capacity has far exceeded our ability to determine what the meanings of these findings are.

The second problem is communicating information before its significance is truly understood. The Chemical Industry Institute of Toxicology (CIIT) was organized some 10 years ago to develop information on the health effects of important commodity chemicals such as benzene and formaldehyde and to conduct basic research in toxicology. The institute very early adopted a policy that test information would be released to the public only after it was complete and subject to peer review by other professionals. (In many cases, these professionals are from academia as well as from the institute and from government.) This has been a credible policy and one that should be a model for research and testing organizations. Too often, new findings are announced before their practical significance can be determined.

However, a very real element of this problem is that companies and communities must deal with accidents immediately. Although advance preparation for such events can help, risk communicators must still deal with explaining an accident and its consequences on the spot. There is not a lot of time for careful analysis, and there is no neat measuring stick such as the Richter Scale to put emergencies and accidents into a rapid, accurate perspective.

The third communication problem concerns industry credibility or lack thereof. For too long, industry in general has viewed risk communication as unnecessary. We have reasoned that our scientists indicate that the risk to the public is insignificant, and that is all that matters. Why should we bother talking about something that is of no concern to anybody else? Many a Dow official has hanging on his or her office wall a sign that reads, "Perception is reality." And in Dow's case, our silence has often created a suspicion that we are hiding something, that we are suppressing important information that should or could affect public health.

When we talk more openly about risk and elaborate, for example, on the chemical industry's outstanding safety record, or the programs society has in place to deal with emergency situations, the public often views such communications with skepticism. People now wonder what ulterior motive or hidden agenda we have in communicating this type of information. And to be sure, we have reasons beyond serving the public interest for effectively communicating risk. But so does everybody else in the risk communication arena—whether the objectives are to sell more products, secure additional research funding, draw public attention, attract more readers or viewers, acquire additional political clout, or merely beat the competition to the punch. Everyone who communicates risk is serving more than just the public interest by doing so.

To summarize, there are three problems that hamper effective risk communication: (1) the difficulty in distinguishing between low and high risks, (2) the communication of information before it is fully understood, and (3) the credibility problem.

I do have a few suggestions for improving risk communication in general. First, the NSF-EPA [National Science Foundation-Environmental Protection Agency] assessment of the literature on risk communication [see Appendix] is very worthwhile. The division of communication into four parts—message, source, channel, and receiver—is very helpful in the design of communication programs. Certainly we must design different strategies for meeting the four basic objectives identified in the study: education, behavioral change, emergency readiness, and issue resolution.

Second, much of science centers on findings that require complex analysis and further study before anyone can determine if there is a need for risk reduction. At Dow we have learned that it is helpful to communicate what we are doing to get more information and to indicate the approximate time at which our study results will be available.

Third, in crises such as a chemical spill or an accident, there are no substitutes for advance planning. Company and industry emergency programs have been in place for many years, and these programs are now being strengthened. For example, the Comprehensive Accident and Emergency Response (CAER) Program of the Chemical Manufacturers Association coordinates emergency planning with local communities and manufacturing sites. As a result, communication will become more timely, will occur as a result of specific objectives and particular events, and will involve more people than in the past.

Finally, as a scientist and a businessman, I have learned that analyzing and discussing the handling of chemical substances with people outside the chemical industry is extremely difficult. Most of us have come out of laboratories as research people, and we are comfortable dealing with other researchers. We are not particularly comfortable working with the public, although many of us, myself included, have learned the hard way in attempting to do this. I have experienced firsthand the difficulty of putting risk into perspective and trying to explain it in practical, lay terms so that people can understand it.

Wouldn't it be productive and beneficial to have some vehicle for bringing all interested parties together to discuss some of the difficulties we are discussing today? Such a team approach might go a long way in helping to depolarize the situation we are in. It would give people with divergent viewpoints an opportunity to present and discuss their views. We heard last night at this conference that we can accomplish a lot more by doing things together and becoming partners in such an approach. This symposium represents an important first step.

Thomas Burke
Assistant Commissioner, Division of Occupational and Environmental Health, New Jersey Department of Health *

New Jersey is a good place to learn about risk communication. It is a state with a very sensitive citizenry, a supportive government, and considerable experience in day-to-day risk communication.

As DEP's director of research, I understand the need for good science and research as well as the need to communicate findings on an individual level. Risk communication is not a new discipline; it is a new name for something we have all been doing for a long time. Nor is risk assessment a new discipline—we have all been making decisions and evaluating risks. However, risk communication and risk assessment both offer a framework that helps us to better express the kinds of things that we have been doing, and to find better ways of making environmental decisions.

One common public perception is that scientists are highly quantitative in their approach to environmental issues. As a scientist, I have to explain to citizen groups what the Ames test does and what carcinogenicity means. Yet scientists also have intense personal encounters with the public. I had to meet with the parents of children who died in a leukemia cluster in Rutherford, New Jersey, in 1977 and explain to them what we knew and, more importantly, what we didn't know. I had to explain to the community and the national networks, *Newsweek* magazine, and so on that we really don't know. I stated that it is safe to go to school, it is safe to live in Rutherford, and I explained what we were doing to address the problem. But one of the things that as scientists we are often afraid to admit is that we don't know.

More research is needed, and that is why we have a vigorous and aggressive research program in New Jersey. I would like to give two quick examples of the need for research and then talk about what we are doing in New Jersey.

New Jersey's two biggest recent environmental issues began as small research initiatives. One of these was dioxin. We began by looking at the issue from a research or method-development perspective. In doing

---

*At the time of the conference, Dr. Burke was Director, Office of Science and Research, New Jersey Department of Environmental Protection (DEP).

our homework we tried to narrow down the most likely spot where we would find dioxin.

We stumbled on a former Agent Orange-producing facility in north New Jersey. The first measurement was 50,000 times the one-part-per-billion number used as a guideline in Times Beach, Missouri. Instantly, a research project turned into a media event. We had the governor, helicopters, and the *New York Post* coming in. We had incredible photo opportunities. It was clearly a case in which there was not time to think through how to communicate risk.

A very important question in risk communication is the timing of data releases. Do you release one fact or several: Do you wait five years until you have a full assessment? There has to be an answer somewhere in the middle, but I do not have that answer. Sound risk communication has to be guided by sound science, and somewhere in the middle there is a place for public participation, there is a place for research, and there is a place for good communication. We have not yet located those places.

And now to my second example—radon. Our encounters with radon in New Jersey are soon to become much more major. I am involved primarily in toxic-substance issues, and radon is a different kind of pollutant. But I have had some recent personal experience with it. In New Jersey people have been living in homes that were actually built on waste from radium processing. I had to call these people the night before the data were to be released to the local health department, and therefore to the press, and explain to them that they had this invisible gas in their basements and that it posed a risk the magnitude of which we had not seen before in toxics investigations. And I had to try to recommend, on a personal level, what these people should do before we really knew what could be done. I had grown men crying on the other end of the phone because they had little babies and they kept their playpens in the basements. How could I, as an epidemiologist, explain to them what radon meant? I could not. I admitted that to the people I spoke with. I could not talk about one-in-a-thousand risk because I did not know the individual risk.

These are the kinds of problems we encounter—problems that are not easily quantifiable. You have to be able to offer opportunities to the public to be involved, to help themselves, or else people will feel completely helpless and you will find yourself in a real quandary as a government representative.

The Reading Prong in New Jersey is a natural formation of radon-producing uranium, and there are over a million buildings sitting on it. We are beginning to take measurements; we are beginning to be very scientific in our approach. In addition, we are also realizing that although we have spent a lot of money in New Jersey cleaning up Superfund sights and so forth, we cannot clean the Reading Prong: it is just not going to happen. The best we can offer is good information, good communication of risk, real involvement of citizens. Nobody put radon in the Reading Prong, which makes the situation somewhat different from a hazardous waste or toxic waste situation. At the same time, the risks are several orders of magnitude higher than we have seen before.

What we have done is to convene a panel of experts, including some among us now, through Dr. Peter Sandman of Rutgers University, to try to develop an approach to this problem. There are things we now understand about radon, and there are ways to go about dealing with it. But just as we researched ways to measure toxic substances in the 1970s, we now have to research how to communicate about radon, because we have learned that there are no risk-free solutions. How clean is clean, and how do we balance the risks?

What we are trying to do in New Jersey is to focus on risk communication issues. The governor, in his recent "state of the state" address, mentioned the formation of a new environmental health assessment program that will help explain risk. In the DEP, we are starting a three-part risk communication research effort. We are looking first at the state of the art. What is out there to help risk communicators? We have 3,000 communicators in the DEP, but no manual for them. We need to develop a common set of tools for our communicators.

We are also looking at public perceptions of risk. Through the Eagleton Institute, we will be polling the public in New Jersey. We need to find out whether we are emphasizing the right things—to take a hard look at the general public in New Jersey so that we can approach it with a clear sense of its perceptions of risk *and* of the agency.

Finally, we are taking a hard look at ourselves. How have we communicated risk in the past? Is it appropriate? And what can we learn from it? Through our combined continued research efforts in risk assessment and this three-point approach to the communication process, we hope to be in much better shape to come to grips with some of these issues and to develop a rational problem-solving approach to environmental issues in New Jersey.

Panel

Trust and Credibility: The Central Issue?

Roger Kasperson, Chairperson
Hazard Assessment Group, Center for Technology, Environment, and Development, Clark University

There is ample evidence that trust and confidence in the risk communication process is not as high as it might be, although no one is sure why this is so. For example, in the EDB [ethylene dibromide] case, we have an image of a beleaguered Environmental Protection Agency (EPA) trying desperately to explain its risk management effort to an obviously skeptical and concerned public. One explanation for diminished public trust in the EPA during this crisis points to the inability of the agency to deal with what have been described as the two worlds of risk assessment. There is the *macro* risk assessment of the expert and the *micro* or subjective risk assessment of the individual—a situation, it has been claimed, that produced confusion and ultimately antagonism toward the agency during the EDB incident. Serious research is needed on this issue so that programs can be developed to deal with public distrust.

We are now in a substantial national effort to site radioactive waste facilities in the United States. The search for sites has uncovered an obvious unwillingness on the part of the public to accept risk statements by the Department of Energy and other responsible authorities. Now, is that unwillingness or skepticism a function of the particular types of hazard involved—that is, the connection between siting risks and nuclear risk more generally? Is the unwillingness connected with the involuntary nature of the risk? Is it a function of the concerns about equity? Does it stem from distrust of the Department of Energy? Is it a function of disagreement among experts? Or does the public's skepticism have to do fundamentally with the question of who is going to have what kinds of decision-making power?

It is interesting to contrast a case such as the EDB crisis with hurricanes. Why is it that the National Hurricane Tracking Center commands such respect and confidence? Again, is it because we are dealing with a familiar hazard that we know, one that many of us have experienced? Is it because hurricanes are a slowly developing hazard that can be seen in the various stages of their evolution? Is it the fact that we have effective visual ways of representing the movement of hurricanes and the kind of danger they present? Or is the trust connected with institutional reasons or with the newscaster who describes it to us so effectively?

In the early 1960s, if you posed a question to the American public about its level of confidence in statements made by industry, churches, various social institutions, or the government, you generally received overwhelmingly positive answers. Two decades later, the public is showing remarkably little confidence in the institutions that impart information—not only the EPA but churches, industry, local government, various kinds of experts, and so forth. There has obviously been a dramatic change in attitudes regarding the trustworthiness of social institutions in general, which is a much broader problem than the specific institutional risk problems we are talking about here.

A second major historical development, which is important and which has been alluded to at several points in this conference, is the growing concern for public health and safety in the United States at a time when almost all the objective measures indicate that we are actually safer. It is important to appreciate the extent to which this conference is a distinctly American phenomenon. It is very much linked to our political culture. We have a difficult risk communication problem partly because we have bureaucrats, rather than the civil servants found in other countries, and partly because we have a process in which participants "fight out" public policy or regulatory issues, rather than searching for consensus. And we have long relished the wisdom of the common person rather than that of the experts in universities, government, and so on.

What is this phenomenon of social trust? One thing is clear—although our understanding of it is poor, like risk perception, trust is multi-dimensional, and it is certainly different for different social groups. There is not a single risk communication problem; there is not a single social trust problem. There are many problems, and they are different.

It has been mentioned several times during this conference that, when we do not know something, we should say so clearly. We must inform the public candidly that we do not know adequately what the risk situation is, or that we are still amassing exposure data. Yet when we say this, we create a problem on another dimension of social trust: people want to believe regulators are competent, and they want to believe that experts have the information and understand the danger. Thus, the more we are candid about what we don't know, the greater the risk that we will be seen as not in control. If, on the other hand, we attempt to show people that we are good scientists, if we make statements as clear and precise as possible and present the best data we have, there is a very good chance that we will erode public perceptions of trust. People will hear experts disagreeing, and they will think, "Why are you taking such a clear position when the evidence is so disputed?" In short, the more that you try to be forthright and provide all the data, the more you may risk appearing uncaring or arrogant.

We need to understand the multidimensional nature of public trust and how it differs for different social groups. To deal with these questions today, we have a distinguished panel. Vernon Houk is the director of the Center for Environmental Health, Centers for Disease Control. Steve Klaidman is a journalist and senior research fellow at the Kennedy Institute of Ethics, Georgetown University. Frances Lynn, from the Institute of Environmental Studies at the University of North Carolina, directs the Environmental Resource Center there. Finally, Peter Sandman is on the faculty of the Department of Journalism at Rutgers University and has extensive experience in the design of various communications programs.

The format for this panel will be somewhat different from that of the preceding one. We have developed a number of questions that we feel are critical in the area of public trust, which we would like to explore. First, why do people trust other people in institutions—what factors are the most important? Second, is it reasonable for experts to ask the public to trust them in risk communication; if not, how do we proceed and with what potential success? Third, to what extent has an overall loss of public confidence and trust in government and social institutions occurred over the past several decades, and what explains this loss? Fourth, to the extent that lack of trust and credibility is a problem, is it primarily a lack of trust in information, or in the institutions and individuals doing the communicating? Fifth, what about the role of the mass media—how do media coverage and presentation affect trust and credibility? Sixth, should risk information ever be withheld from the public—and if so, under what conditions? And seventh, is it possible to establish guidelines for risk communication that would increase trust and credibility? If so, what would they look like?

I would like to begin with the first question, which I will pose to Steve Klaidman. Why do people trust other people in institutions; what factors do you see as important?

Steve Klaidman: There are a variety of factors. People begin operating with the assumption that things will go well. When they fail to go well, nearly any institution associated with the failure, whether or not that institution is responsible, suffers a loss of trust and credibility. But there are obviously many overlapping factors. One of the few conclusive poll results is that anchormen on television are trusted. What is the significance of this? Because people see a familiar face on television every night, because the anchorman reads the news in a relatively authoritative fashion and most of the time it is right, it becomes acceptable. The news becomes the truth, and the public finds it trustworthy.

Yet there is clearly a tremendous amount of ambiguity involved in the whole question of trust—ambiguity in such areas as the nature of risk, the nature of the risk communications process, and the nature of institutions. At certain times, certain institutions are regarded as trustworthy, at other times they are not—again, largely as a result of the way events turn out. The media are now rated higher in many polls of public trust than are business or just about any other institution. There is no good reason for that to be so.

Roger Kasperson: Vernon [Houk], you are part of an institution with a lot of experience that differs greatly from the press. Could you comment?

Vernon Houk: Yes. Trust in an institution is based on the record of what happens or does not happen. We might look back at the beginning of this century and the last century, at our efforts to provide safe drinking water and foods. If these were not safe, people became sick. If people did not get sick, that was evidence that something had been accomplished. What we are talking about now, however, particularly with regard to low-dose, chronic exposures to toxic materials, are risks that probably cannot be measured above background levels in almost all instances.

In this context, I would like to comment on two particular words used in the preceding panel. One is the word *accident*. I think it is a terrible mistake to use this word. These are not accidents—although they are not intentional, they are incidents that have a cause. Accident implies a random event that cannot be controlled. The other word is *victims*. Populations around a toxic waste site or a population that may have been exposed to a material that may or may not produce adverse health effects have been referred to as victims. I think that you are prejudging the situation and not allowing the scientific dialogue enough time to decide whether or not these people are in fact victims.

Roger Kasperson: Ellen Silbergeld, I wonder if you might comment on what produces trust in [your organization,] EDF [Environmental Defense Fund]?

Ellen Silbergeld: One of the critical issues of trust, and what promotes trust, relates to the question of action versus inaction, and of presence— of being present and responsive when something is demanded. Trust is something that we all know is slow to build but very quick to dissipate. It is interesting to note the relative ease of [the EPA in] communicating decisions recently taken on asbestos as compared with the morass of miscommunication over EDB. We might consider the typology of those two decisions before we get enmeshed in considering the communication that took place around them. In the public's mind there is a record of things done, which is then balanced against a record of things not done. And the public keeps a very good count. You will be in trouble if you start falling behind, not in terms of extreme or severe regulatory controls, but in terms of the perception that you are doing something— taking action rather than looking for reasons for not taking action.

Dr. [Etcyl] Blair mentioned earlier that science is very good at providing reasons for our hesitancy. We must not get caught up in that. At scientific meetings people do not get caught up in that. They do not end up their papers by saying that more research is needed and therefore we do not know anything about the subject. On any hotly contested scientific issue, scientists are proposing all kinds of conclusions, actions, steps to be taken, possible therapies, etiologic explanations. The issue of trust is really related to your actions; people do judge you on your actions more than your words, and when your actions fail they distrust your words.

Roger Kasperson: Frances Lynn, given that you work with citizen groups, what does effective action mean to you?

Frances Lynn: I think coaction is the answer. One very important factor in trust is the autonomy of the person with whom you are trying to communicate. Research suggests that one thing a doctor can do to break trust with his or her patient is to lie to that person. I think lying and the issue of autonomy are very closely linked—that when you take away from another person the right to make his or her own decision, when you make a decision without involving him or her, the result is negative. Trust is not an issue for government or industry alone. It is a matter of very active listening to diverse groups, of involving people in the planning of activities.

Roger Kasperson: Let's move on to the next question. Peter Sandman, is it reasonable for experts to ask the public to trust them in risk communication? If not, what are we doing?

Peter Sandman: There is one sense in which it is obviously reasonable for experts to want and expect to be trusted. Most experts are trained professionals. They see themselves as overworked, underpaid, and socially responsible. And it is certainly human for an expert who is trying desperately hard to serve the public to want, if not the public's gratitude, at least the public's trust. Much of the frigidity with which experts interact with hostile publics is basically hurt feelings or suppressed anger.

Yet, in another sense I think it is terribly unreasonable and dysfunctional for experts to want to be trusted; this desire gets in the way of what I take to be the task of this conference, which is to figure out how to do a better job of getting the public to understand more about risk.

I want to put this in learning theory terms. There are basically three circumstances in which people learn well. One is when they are curious, which is a motivation that we have reason to believe diminishes considerably after about the age of 11. That leaves two others. One is what social scientists call postdecisional distance-reduction—in other words, learning that is a very biased kind of information seeking, a search for ammunition to support a particular point of view. This is presumably not what we are complaining about when we complain that the public is not learning properly about risk.

The only other circumstance in which people really learn well is a predecisional one—when they face the need to make a decision and they have a rational reason for wanting to decide wisely. This raises the issue of power, which is terribly important. We present the public often, it seems to me, with a really irrational demand. We say, "We are going to decide what is to be done and we want you to approve of our decision, so please listen carefully, think deeply, and attend to the nuances. Of course, we are not going to pay the least bit of attention to what you say, but please be wise." And people are not thoughtful in their learning if they have no power to affect the outcome of decisions.

In a sense, when we ask to be trusted, we are really saying, "Listen carefully and do whatever we say." Well, if people are going to do whatever we say, they do not have to listen carefully. When the public has power, an opportunity to meaningfully contribute to a decision as to what is to be done, then it becomes extraordinarily good at understanding probability and uncertainty, at grappling with the complexities of risk. In asking to be trusted we make a very serious mistake. If we would trust the public more and ask to be trusted less, citizens would understand a great deal more of what we have to say.

Roger Kasperson: Does he have it right, Steve [Klaidman]?

Steve Klaidman: Well, I thought he was going in a slightly different direction. The public understands, among other things, that experts are professionals, but also that they are frequently interested parties. I think a tremendous amount of the public's distrust results from the fact that the public sees experts' interests at play and makes its decisions about whether to trust experts on that basis. Sometimes the interested parties are as unbiased as can be, and they produce the best-quality information presented in the clearest possible way; but that does not really get to the problem of trust. Distrust still remains because of the question of interests.

Roger Kasperson: Frances [Lynn]?

Frances Lynn: I want to speak to both these issues and what we can do about them. North Carolina has provided funding for citizen groups along with their local governments to hire experts to work with the citizens in assessing risks at the local level. The citizens have become document readers; they draw on the expertise in the community and learn very quickly. There are mechanisms available, including providing funding so that citizen groups and local governments can select their own experts or reach some kind of consensus on who would be acceptable to everyone.

Roger Kasperson:Would you like to comment, [Alvin Alm]?

Alvin Alm: Yes. In listening to this discussion I am impressed with how imprecise we are when we talk about the public. If you are talking about a regulatory action at the national level, what you basically have is a number of elite groups—industry, environmental groups, trade associations; you do not really have the public. We have to be a lot more precise about what we mean when we talk about involving the public. Are we talking about opinion polls? At local sites we can involve the public to some extent, but I am not sure that in any particular case we are really reaching out to a broad span of public opinion. Moreover, if the question is one of alternative sites or removing wastes from one place to another, we are never representing those people who have the waste problem now. We have to think very carefully about what we mean by the public if we are really going to get at the question of how to communicate with the public.

Roger Kasperson: Vernon Houk, much of the discussion so far has focused on what rights the public has, how various publics might be involved, and so forth. What about the expert? Do you, as someone in the Centers for Disease Control, feel you have a right to be trusted in statements that you make?

Vernon Houk: Not unless my statements are reasonable. Trust is not necessarily credibility, and you have to have trust and credibility. I think that most of us can think of a few people who are trusted by the general public but who have very little scientific credibility. One of the ways that we can have trust from people is to speak in terms that they can understand. Scientists frequently become so scientifically precise that no one knows what they are talking about.

I will give an example: the dioxin incident at the Boy Scout jamboree*. It caused major public hysteria. One poison center kept releasing, every two hours, a statement of what people should do; it had no information upon which to make any statements. We finally concluded, very rapidly, that in our opinion no harm had been done. I think people could understand that. If we had said that it was our opinion that the cancer risk was less than one in 60 million, we still would have had everybody saying, "But I am the one!"

Trust results when we communicate in ways that are understandable to people.

Roger Kasperson: Peter [Sandman], a question to you: Vernon [Houk] has just made an argument that we ought to proceed in ways that rebuild or capture trust. I heard you saying something quite different, which is that we ought to proceed without any expectation that trust will be there. How do we do that, and with what success? How do you operate if there is no trust in the atmosphere? Is there going to be any risk communication success in such a situation?

Peter Sandman: I would both agree and disagree with what Vernon [Houk] is saying. Certainly it is important not to use jargon as a defense against the public. One of the things we did on the Kemeny Commission that I thought was very interesting was to analyze for language complexity, the sources' conversations with each other and the sources' conversations with reporters. What we found was there was more jargon and much more complex language when engineers were talking to the public than when engineers were talking to other engineers. That is very

---

*Editor's note: On November 9, 1984, the Department of the Army announced that dioxin-containing material had been stored near the site of the 1981 jamboree.

clear evidence that jargon was a defense, and that cultivates distrust. But ultimately it seems to me important to notice that people can master extremely technical language, full of detail, if they are motivated to do so. My answer to what we should do to be trustworthy is perhaps an end run around the question, but I think it is important. We will be trusted as sources if we work in a universe in which our audiences have reason to listen—in which they have a motive for wanting to know what we have to say. By and large, by being reluctant to share control over decisions with them, we deprive them of that motive. I think that is the chief reason why we are not trusted.

Roger Kasperson: I wonder what this problem looks like from inside a large chemical company, Mr. [Etcyl] Blair. You have found yourself, obviously, in situations of being forced to operate in contexts with relatively low levels of trust. How do you manage those situations? Is it possible to be successful?

Etcyl Blair: I would answer the first question: with difficulty. The primary institution that we are geared to deal with is the federal government. We do not operate only one plant in this country, we do not produce only one product; in fact, there are very few activities about which we have not supplied, in some manner or another, a fair amount of information to the federal government and many of its agencies. The [chemical] companies are prepared to take information to the technical groups within those agencies. Where we get into problems, of course, is with the public, because generally a particular public is not that tuned into technical detail. The scientists who are called upon to give expert opinions deal in technical matters and language, which creates difficulties with communication.

Roger Kasperson: Let's move on to the next question. Frances [Lynn], to what extent do you see an overall loss of public confidence or trust in government and social institutions in the United States, and how serious is it? What do you see as its sources?

Frances Lynn: The fact that we are dealing here with the issue of trust is a step forward, but it comes at the end of a series of trust-diminishing incidents. Bill Ruckelshaus started out by pointing to Watergate and

Vietnam. We are looking now at the findings of the Atomic Energy Commission and the cover-up of the Nevada tests, which came out in the press in the late 1970s; lawsuits were won, and people discovered that they had been lied to. That diminishes trust. We are now talking about asbestos victims. Testimony came out in the asbestos trial in which corporate officials were described as saying, "Do not tell them, it will frighten them," and we find that same message among coal miners and cotton dust workers. There are reasons for the mistrust.

My main concern is that I see communication as a mechanism for accomplishing something or conveying something, but what we are not talking about is what we wish to accomplish or to convey. We no longer have a consensus on what that is, although at one time we thought we had (particularly in the area of the environment). Until we can get back to talking about what we want to accomplish, discussing the communication process will not get us anywhere—it would be as if we had invented the world's most perfect television set and had nothing new to show on it. One of the fundamental issues is a loss of trust, but that is not going to be regained by designing better television sets, so to speak.

Roger Kasperson: Al Alm, you made the comment at the end of the last panel that you are really not very optimistic about this undertaking, or what might come out of it, in terms of actual risk communication programs. Is your discouragement connected with some broad social issues? Could you comment on why you feel that way?

Alvin Alm: I am pessimistic for three reasons. First, there are two languages being spoken—that of the regulator and that of the average citizen. The language of the regulator does describe risk assessment, but most people do not understand or at least do not think in relativistic terms; hence regulators and people end up talking across and not to each other. I have rarely heard a good dialogue between citizens and government officials on risk assessment. The government people tend to have their minds pretty much closed, and vice versa. Second, the public's latent distrust of government, for the reasons we have already talked about, makes risk communication difficult. And third, the institutional setting for decisions on risks is one established not for national communications but for highlighting dramatic differences, which leads not to public understanding but to confusion. On any particular issue a government regulatory agency will come out with a decision that will be attacked immediately by all groups, as being either too strong or too weak. The media will issue a one-liner to the effect that the decision is being attacked by environmentalists or industry or whatever, and the public will be conveyed a message. It is thus difficult for the public to have a clear idea of what kind of risks government agencies are dealing with, and government officials in turn have a difficult time communicating their decisions in this kind of institutional setting.

Tom Burke: Maybe when you are dealing with problems on a federal level pessimism is warranted, but I do not think that a panel of experts should be up here saying they are pessimistic. We have to be committed to a course of action. In New Jersey, much of that course is determined, not by toxicologists but by the will of the people. I hear people saying that there is no research on risk communication, but that is not true. I hear people saying that no new look is being taken at hazardous waste problems; that, too, is not true. There are possibilities for movement on these issues, and I have seen it happen. I realize there are no immediate solutions, but I am not pessimistic. Communication will not in itself bring about change, yet perhaps the best vehicle for initiating change is a more effective way of communicating risks. Of course, we must develop the public's trust. When, for instance, the EPA comes out with a guideline, does the state government accept it and put it into practice? No; we evaluate it, we have a give-and-take. That is the scientific method, and technical and bureaucratic method for getting things done. And yet, for some reason, as regulators we do not grant citizens that same right. We expect blind acceptance of our decisions and are naturally met with mistrust. Until we involve citizens in the decision-making process, perhaps through improved peer review with citizen involvement, government officials are not going to have the public level of trust we would like them to have.

Roger Kasperson: Etcyl [Blair]?

Etcyl Blair: Yes. I think we must proceed with optimism, because increasingly our professional, technical people are learning how to deal with the public. They participate in various kinds of forums, and they are learning how to be comfortable doing that. We [Dow Chemical] put a lot more effort now into becoming a better-understood company. At one time nobody knew anything about us as a company; as a result, we encountered some great difficulties later on with a series of products. It is very important that the public knows that we are producing chemical products, the value that these products have and their possible associated risks, the jobs that are involved, the competition between our company and another company, and the competition between the United States and other parts of the world. Even scientists in the Dow Chemical Company are public citizens; we too want to get this communication process going.

Alvin Alm: Let me just make this short observation. This country has made a tremendous effort to involve people in decisions that affect their lives, particularly at the local level, and I applaud that. But this is somewhat different from risk communication, which is a more difficult problem because you are dealing with the questions of the people who are actually communicating, and you need to understand different kinds of languages, different bases for looking at things. That is why I am pessimistic about the communication process—but I think the nation *is* making great progress in terms of openness and involving people in decisions.

Peter Sandman: It is useful to consider for a moment what journalists mean by trust. Reporters trust you if they know which axe you are grinding. They figure you are grinding it with integrity. They do not demand that you not have an axe, only that it be visible and that you grind it without lying too outrageously. If we redefine trust in this way, we can behave more trustworthily. What that requires is, I think, exactly what Tom Burke is talking about. You say what you have to say, and you say it up front; you acknowledge the viewpoint, the convictions, the commitments that your statements come from, be it an industry commitment or an environmentalist commitment or a regulatory commitment. You acknowledge that up front. You ask the public not to trust that you have the truth but that you have *a* truth, a point of view honestly presented. That is a trust that we can merit.

Roger Kasperson: Tom [Vacor].

Tom Vacor: In my view Americans are basically a trusting people—or to put it another way, they have no reason not to trust you until you give them a reason. One of the media's functions has been to provide lots of reasons not to trust people. Certain industries and professions are not going to be held in high esteem by the media, and since we decide what is news, we have a great capacity for doing damage.

There is an industry distrust list circulating in the media. The oil industry is not trusted; I suspect a lot of that has to do with what happened in the early 1970s. The nuclear industry is not trusted. The automobile industry, specifically the Detroit-based U.S. manufacturers, is not trusted by consumers at all, And the government is not well trusted for a variety of reasons; probably the best reasons would be Vietnam and then Watergate.

So who do we trust? Well, we have a tendency to trust environmentalists, primarily because they buck moneyed interests and generally they have little money to do so. They tend to be remarkably educated and remarkably skilled at using the media. We trust scientists, but not necessarily those of the corporate or government stripe, simply because we feel they have an extra axe to grind. But if we find an independent science educator, that person is likely to get a lot of press.

Roger Kasperson: A quick comment?

Frances Lynn: One issue that is skirted is the question of the size of institutions, which may be a reason for some of the pessimism at the federal level and optimism at the local level. There is a very good article about mediating institutions, written by Peter Berger and published by the American Enterprise Institute a few years ago. Berger suggests that whether the institution is big government, a big labor union, or a big corporation, it will have a problem, and the problem is that it is taking decision-making power away from the citizen. There has to be some sensitivity to this problem: whether the government is liberal or conservative, it is big, and the same thing holds for corporations. Effort must then be directed toward working through mediating institutions.

Roger Kasperson: One obvious question comes out of this. To the extent that there are long-run historical factors that have detracted from social trust; to the extent that institutions are better able to expose differences of opinion than to engage in risk communication; and given the historical loss of confidence in social institutions, what is the prospect of success for the various people sitting in the audience who may be involved in designing individual risk communication programs aimed at recapturing a certain amount of social trust? Is there much to be gained from an individual program, however well designed and well intentioned, when we have these longer-run historical trends and deeper structural problems?

Tom Vacor: I will take a whack at that question because I can give you an excellent example of how an individual program could have been useful. In 1979, a DC-10 took off from Chicago; its engine fell off and many people were killed. McDonnell Douglas Corporation made the most ignorant blunder that it had ever made: it buried its head in the sand. It wanted to protect its employees and American Airlines. The truth of the matter was that the engine was designed to break off; if the airplane landed with the wheels up, the engine would break off and fly over the wings so that it would not come up through the wing, puncture the fuel tanks, and burn all the passengers up.

The problem was that McDonnell Douglas chose not to talk about that; it chose to put its head in the sand. It built many fewer DC-10s than it might have built, and it is only now starting to build them again because there is a need for wide-bodies. Yet many people will not fly on the new airplane because they are afraid that the engine is going to fall off. By choosing not to talk about the design, the company did itself great damage.

Roger Kasperson: Etcyl Blair, at the end of the last panel, I thought I heard you making a fairly persuasive argument for certain conditions under which risk information ought to be withheld from the public. Did I hear you right?

Etcyl Blair: That is right—you hear very well! What I was suggesting is that risk assessment is going on all the time. Every experiment carried out at the Dow Chemical Company somehow conveys information. But we do not run the results of every experiment to the EPA; we do not run them to the news media. As we develop a product or process, or develop information, there comes an appropriate time when we must take this information either to an agency or to our customers, or we must do something with it. In certain instances where the information concerns public health and the environment, there are certain legal requirements for reporting the information. But information has to be managed—you do not just yell "fire." We have some responsibility to manage it; sometimes we do not do this well. I hope we will do it better in the future than we have in the past, but we just do not run our information down Main Street every day.

Roger Kasperson: Peter [Sandman], unless I have misread some of your writings, I would not expect you to be in the same place on this issue.

Peter Sandman: No, on the whole I do not agree. It is possible to construct a scenario where the responsible thing to do would be to withhold information, but I think this would be a very extreme and very unlikely scenario. In the real world the problem we encounter far more often is the withholding of information for understandable internal reasons— information that it would be wise to announce. I was impressed, during the Three Mile Island incident, with the one organization that came out of that public information debacle with a decent reputation: the state health department. During the first two weeks after Three Mile Island, the state health department released a daily announcement that went something like this: "We have tested the milk for iodine 131. We have not found any. We are surprised; we thought we would find some. We are going to test it again tomorrow. We still advise against drinking the milk." At the end of those two weeks, when the health department stated that there was no iodine 131 in the milk, their statement was universally believed. And it was believed because the department had been willing to release very tentative data; it had announced the extent to which it believed or did not believe its own findings.

Right now, New Jersey is confronting a problem with radon, which Tom Burke talked about. And there are very good reasons for not going public right now, because we do not know very much about how many homes are exposed and to what levels, and we know even less about what remedial actions should be taken. The temptation to withhold information is overwhelming. But if New Jersey does that, I predict with absolute certainty that three or four years from now, when the state announces the extent of the risk and what people ought to do, residents will want to know how long the state has known about the risks. The state will reply "We have been studying radon for three years." And residents will say, "So for three years you have let me keep my children in a cancer-infested, dangerous place, and you did not bother to tell me about it!" There will be a huge loss of credibility.

To its credit, the New Jersey government does not intend to do that. It intends to launch a proactive information campaign. Even though the information is incomplete, even though the state is not at all certain what people ought to do about radon or what the risk is, its officials are telling residents what they know as they learn it. This approach has its real costs—people thinking, "My God, aren't you experts ever going to figure out the answer?" Yet I think we are a lot better off with the public wondering why we do not know the answer than with the pubic wondering why we knew the answer and waited to tell them.

Roger Kasperson: Steve Klaidman?

Steve Klaidman: There is an important distinction to be drawn between not releasing and withholding information. There can be information overkill about risk as well as anything else, and clearly if Dow Chemical or any other company were to release all its information on chemicals, nobody would know what to do with it. We would be buried in it. At the same time, I agree with Peter [Sandman]. When there is vital information, as in the case of radon, it is far better to get that information out in some form, so that people can deal with it in some way. It is better to run the lesser risk of having people confused or even panicked in some cases, rather than the greater risk of having them find out three weeks, three months, or a year later that certain information was known and was withheld.

Roger Kasperson: Vernon [Houk]?

Vernon Houk: I would agree, as long as we can provide some information on mitigation, or actions that people can take. But I would like to add to this question. As distasteful as withholding information from the public is, is it not equally as distasteful and destructive to scare the public and to give people information that is far beyond what we actually know? From 1978 until the present, unfortunately, many people have been unable to use dioxin without thinking of it as the most toxic substance known to humans. And we have a whole list of these things. What is the appropriate balance? We should not withhold significant information, nor should we terrify everybody.

Roger Kasperson: Now to the last and toughest question. Is it possible to establish guidelines for risk communication that would increase trust and credibility? If so, what would they look like? Frances [Lynn].

Frances Lynn: We need to bring together the citizens who may be affected by certain substances or events, along with regulators and industry representatives, so they can all sit down, and look at cases, identify the major issues, and establish in advance ethical, credible, and trustworthy ways to react to potential crisis situations.

Roger Kasperson: Any other reactions to that question?

Ellen Silbergeld: Well, I am struck by the question because, generally speaking, information will out. It is very difficult to successfully conceal information; to withhold it or to keep it under advisement—whatever terms we want to use, but let's say delay its release for whatever reason—is very difficult to do. And because of this fact, you must consider the disadvantage of the information's appearing at a time other than when you had planned, and what that does to public trust and to the structures of communication. I think rapidity is a very important hallmark of successful communication. What we have seen with the [explosion of the] space shuttle is exemplary: there has been a very rapid release of information. Whatever is known, even if it is conflicting or way off-base, should be conveyed by a number of sources; it is a mistake to delay until more or "final" information is achieved.

I do not see an overwhelming amount of information in the area of toxic chemicals or hazardous waste, for instance. We are not so filled with information that we are having a difficult time clearing the table and understanding what is going on. I would very seriously differ with Dr. [Etcyl] Blair. I think we need a lot more information from all sources so that we can start to sort it out and evaluate it. It is not really information overload that is killing us but rather a paucity of information;

and because of that paucity (and regardless of its sources), all kinds of misinformation arise.

Alvin Alm: I would like to respond to that. I too favor more information. There is much that needs to be done in terms of developing more data. We will accomplish this only after we set priorities, when we try to do that which is most important first. In this country there has been much redoing of the same things, often because of litigation.

We do need more information. And we are committed to developing that information; we are committed to supplying it to the appropriate agencies and to the people who need it. The more that we can get experts to commit to this process, the sooner we will have the information everyone needs.

Tom Vacor: I would like to suggest three standards. Two of them are aimed at sources of information, and the third is aimed at the media. My first recommendation for the sources, based on the discussion that we have just had, is for them to tell everything they know—tell more than they know, but do it with uncertainty. That is, sources should say, "Here is what we think is going on, here is what we are pretty sure of, here is what is very uncertain but we will know more next Thursday."

My second recommendation, also to sources, is to give people a reason to listen: give them enough power and enough say in the decision-making process that they will be interested in what you know—they will feel they have a stake in listening thoughtfully.

And finally, to the media—and this speaks to a point that we really have not dealt with thoroughly—I recommend the following: look more for the middle. The media tend to define the middle as the merger of two extremes. In an article, there may be two paragraphs saying that a certain chemical is good for you, and two paragraphs saying it will kill you. What tends to be missing in media coverage is enough attention to the middle—to sources who are saying, "Well, the chemical is dangerous, but not as dangerous as some other things," and who give a reasoned, rounded view. One reason for this is that people with reasoned and rounded views are the least likely to want to appear in the media; they are the most reclusive sources. But the recommendation I would make to the media is to seek out these people and give the middle as much attention as the two extremes.

Roger Kasperson: A final comment, Al [Alm]?

Alvin Alm: Well, I was going to make a suggestion for further research, which is probably a good way to end this panel. Considerable thought should be given to the entire institutional setting of risk communication and to whether neutral sources of information are one way of improving risk communication. To assist the problem of credibility, we may need neutral sources. These could be universities or other kinds of nonprofit organizations that would provide believable information in which the public would have higher confidence.

Roger Kasperson: I would like to thank this panel for its collective wisdom and our audience for its kind attention.

Case Studies of Risk Communication

Introduction

Vincent T. Covello, Chairperson
Director, Risk Assessment Program, National Science Foundation

In my introduction, I would like to briefly summarize what I believe are some of the main conclusions of the four case studies that follow. First, the cases illustrate the usefulness of subdividing risk communication problems into problems with the message, with the sender or source, with the channel, and with the receiver. I would like to mention something about each of these aspects. First, message problems.

It was clear in each of the four cases that there were problems with the message itself—deficiencies in scientific understanding, in data, in models, and in methods. These deficiencies resulted in large uncertainties in risk estimates. It was also clear that many of the highly technical analyses cited in the case studies were unintelligible to the average lay person.

There were also source problems, that is, problems associated with the senders of risk information. These included disagreements among experts; resource, legal, and institutional constraints on officials; gaps between societal level aggregate data, generated by government agencies and individual fears and concerns, such as the question in the EDB case, "Can we eat the bread?" And finally, communicators frequently failed to disclose and discuss limitations of risk assessments and the resulting uncertainties.

Among source problems, one particular problem seemed to dominate all others, and that was the lack of trust and credibility. This particular issue appears to have been a major factor in all four cases. The case studies suggest two actions that can be taken to help in this regard. First is the importance of being candid and honest; the importance of being ready, able, and willing, without being coerced, to be forthcoming and to reveal truthfully all that is known or believed about the issue. Second is the importance of decisiveness, of quick and responsible action in accordance with the perceived mandate of the agency. The message is: he who hesitates is lost.

Among channel problems, many tend to focus on deficiencies in the media, including selective and biased media reporting; media emphasis on drama, wrongdoing, disagreements, and conflict; premature disclosure of information; and oversimplification, distortions, and inaccuracy in interpreting and translating technical risk information. Although these problems were mentioned in the four case studies, they were among the least emphasized. I think that this sin of omission is revealing, given the common perception that the media are major contributors to risk communication problems. The lack of consideration and emphasis given to this issue was curious, to say the least. It may be that many of the shortcomings of the media are only a mirror of our own failures as communicators rather than a major source of risk communication problems.

With respect to receiver problems, a number of issues were mentioned in the case studies, including inaccurate perceptions of levels of risk by the public, lack of interest in risk issues by large segments of the population, strong beliefs and opinions that are highly resistant to change, exaggerated expectations of the effectiveness of regulatory actions, the desire for scientific certainty, and a reluctance to make trade-offs between different types of risk or between risks, costs, and benefits.

The case studies, I believe, reveal several ways that risk communicators can improve their performance and be more effective. First, it is important that risk communicators know and be clear about the nature of their problem and about the objectives of the communication. For example, it appears to be essential that communicators be clear in their own mind about whether their role is that of a facilitator or a promoter.

Second, it appears to be critical that communicators use simple and nontechnical language in communicating with the public. For example, it is extremely important to use, to the greatest extent possible, easily understandable graphic and other visual material.

Third, and most important, it is essential that communicators listen to their multiple audiences and know the audience's concerns. The case studies reveal that the heart of effective communication is negotiation and coalition building, not manipulation. But effective negotiation and coalition building are impossible if the parties involved are not clearly recognized or heard.

Risk Factors for Cardiovascular Disease: Cholesterol, Salt, and High Blood Pressure

Panel Chairperson:
David McCallum
Senior Fellow, Institute for Health Policy Analysis, Georgetown University

The relationship of blood pressure, salt, cholesterol, and cardiovascular disease poses a significant problem in terms not only of risk but also of communicating that risk to the public. High blood pressure affects approximately 20 percent of the population. A portion of that population can benefit from reduced sodium in the diet. It is estimated that about 25 percent of the population has cholesterol levels for which experts would recommend some kind of intervention in terms of dietary change. The problem is that there are many other intervening factors that make it difficult to infer personal risk from statistical risk; genetics, lifestyle, the levels of the risk factors, and various other characteristics of individuals can cause their susceptibility to risk to vary.

The technical data on which to base the message about risk are a complex blend drawn from laboratory experiments, animal studies, epidemiologic studies, and clinical trials. The message has evolved over decades of scientific investigation. Even here where the data are good, interpretations differ. There is consensus that risk factors should be of concern, but exactly who should be treated and how, and recommendations for the public at large, are still debated.

For instance, controversy exists over whether low-fat diets, which have been encouraged as a means of reducing the risk of both cardio-vascular disease and cancer, are appropriate for children. Some have suggested that such diets may actually be detrimental to a child's growth and development. Some also feel that it is inappropriate to recommend such diets for the entire population if only certain high-risk groups benefit. Others feel that all will benefit from lowering fat intake. Providing risk information along with information to assist individuals in decision making and behavioral change is the challenge.

The risk communication process in this case study is complicated by social and cultural factors that affect dietary choices, risk perception factors (some people accept higher levels of self-imposed risk), and behavioral factors that make sacrificing short-term pleasures for long-term benefits difficult. The process is aided, however, by the fact that individuals can act directly to reduce their exposure to risk. For the process to be effective, the public must be aware of the risk, have knowledge and skills for appropriate action, and receive positive reinforcement for appropriate behavior. Information must flow through multiple channels, including the popular media, health professionals, and peers.

Cardiovascular risk reduction is a risk communication success story. Increases in awareness and knowledge of risk factors have been documented, as have actual changes in behavior (an increased percentage of the population trying to decrease salt intake, and more hypertensives seeking treatment). Encouraging lower fat and cholesterol consumption is more difficult, but fat in the American diet has decreased. A comprehensive, coordinated program has just been initiated by the Heart, Lung, and Blood Institute to encourage lowering of cholesterol levels. Direct effects of media campaigns to reduce risk factors have been documented in studies by the Stanford Heart Disease Prevention Program [1977]. Perhaps most important, mortality rates from strokes and coronary artery disease have decreased in recent years.

The panel discussing this case study identified a number of specific approaches that panel members believe have contributed to this success. Coalitions and networks involving as many groups as possible have become one of the hallmarks of success. Ensuring that all the groups within the network send complementary rather than conflicting messages promotes a synergistic effect on the recipients. Fostering local involvement and using multiple channels of communication, including TV, radio, doctors' offices, grocery stores, and newspapers, has proved useful in the campaigns that have been mounted so far. In addition to involving the appropriate groups and using the appropriate channels, the panel emphasized the need for continuing reinforcement. Messages about risk need to be sent and heard on a daily basis.

Efforts to educate the public about the health risks posed by dietary salt intake provide a clear example of the various factors contributing to the success of such programs. By enlisting the support and assistance of the food industry, the Food and Drug Administration was able to effect changes in both the supply and labeling of low-sodium products, thereby making behavioral change easier. Additionally, the message to be conveyed was simple, and there was considerable scientific consensus behind it. Because messages about the effect of cholesterol may be slightly different, depending on whether they are aimed at heart disease or cancer, and because there are powerful political lobbies protecting the dairy and meat industries, panelists expressed concern that changes in individuals' intake of cholesterol would be more difficult to achieve.

Despite these notable successes and seemingly effective strategies, the panelists identified a number of remaining challenges to communication in this area. Primary among them is the difficulty of simplifying complex scientific material for messages. For example, using cutoff points to define hypertension and hypercholesteremia helps individuals think about their risk but can also make people too comfortable if they are within the "normal" range or despondent if they slightly exceed it. Panelists suggested moving toward the use of the concept of relative risk to provide the public with a better understanding of the danger presented by various risk factors.

A second challenge is setting priorities for communicating various messages. Because of the increasing attention given to health risks of all kinds, panelists noted the potential for overwhelming the public. Individuals may become jaded in the face of constant reminders of potentially harmful environmental agents or lifestyle choices, and they may lose faith in their ability to significantly reduce such risks. Bearing this in mind when developing campaigns directed at specific risk factors can help to ensure that either the greatest risks or those most amenable to reduction are addressed. Moreover, these campaigns must recognize overall nutrition and the interaction of dietary factors. (For example, not drinking milk to avoid fat rather than drinking low-fat milk can lead to calcium deficiencies.)

Many of the lessons learned in communicating risks related to cholesterol, salt, and high blood pressure can be directly applied to other areas in which behavior must be changed to decrease risk, such as the use of seat belts. The panel stressed that in addition to identifying strategies that appear to be the most successful in eliciting changes in behavior, a more thorough understanding of the actual process by which individuals respond to risk messages, and then change their behavior, would enhance the effectiveness of risk communication.

Hazardous Waste Siting: The Massachusetts Experience

Panel Chairperson:
Joanne Kauffman
Environmental Policy Consultant*

The Massachusetts Hazardous Waste Siting Act has been tested five times in six years. The first three proposals were formally accepted as feasible and deserving of review by the state's Hazardous Waste Facility Siting Council, and a fourth was never acted on. These four proposals were withdrawn in the face of persistent local opposition.

Although some would say that the failure to site a facility since the passage of the law in 1980 is a failure of the act itself, many would argue that the law was successful in preventing four unsound proposals from going forward.

The fifth proposal was in the development phase when the company, Clean Harbors, Inc., of Kingston, Massachusetts, decided to withdraw from Taunton, the proposed community, and to consider alternative sites. This happened despite a carefully constructed communications approach by the company and the state, which led to local respect for the developer and media support for the proposal to have a fair hearing under the provisions of the siting act.

This panel attempted to describe the communication process

---

*At the time of the conference, Ms. Kauffman was Deputy Commissioner, Massachusetts Department of Environmental Management (DEM).

71

implemented in this case and to examine what went wrong despite all that went right in Taunton.

The level of conference participants' interest in this particular discussion was not insignificant. More than two-thirds of the conferees attended this panel—a clear demonstration of the intense interest in risk communication in adversarial situations. This is not surprising. In the last five years, not one new hazardous waste treatment facility has been built in the country, despite many attempts. (In Arizona and Colorado, sitings have occurred but there has been no construction to date; in Ohio and North Carolina, construction is blocked by pending court cases.) Four sitings are now meeting strenuous opposition. In the last seven years, only two new facilities to treat hazardous waste have been sited and built.

The Clean Harbors proposal to site a solvent recovery facility in the Taunton Industrial Park was the first to surface since the second administration of Governor Michael S. Dukakis launched its new five-point program to deal with hazardous waste management in 1983. The cornerstones of this program are cleanup, strict enforcement, waste minimization and source reduction, public participation and education, and siting of necessary facilities. Under Commissioner [James] Gutensohn, the state's Department of Environmental Management (DEM) studied the previous four attempts in the context of the state's need for hazardous waste treatment. The DEM determined that the siting process could work, that Massachusetts needed smaller targeted facilities, and that the most urgently needed facility was one for solvent recovery. In early 1984, Gutensohn delivered a speech outlining the administration's strategy to foster public awareness of the need for solvent recovery in Massachusetts and the methods of treatment, and to identify and attract a good solvent recovery firm. Gutensohn said that, in addition to a good company with a thoughtful proposal, the siting would require the commitment of state level, local, and regional leadership and support from industry.

This strategy assumed that problems in siting originate prior to the developer's official filing of a Notice of Intent and that public education and participation is necessary in both the selection of a company and the shaping of any proposal to meet the state's hazardous waste management needs.

As institutional facilitator of the state's siting process, the DEM carefully screened prospective developers and developed a program to fund regional coalitions across the state to address hazardous waste management issues. The aim of the program was to foster better understanding of the issues by strengthening grass-roots efforts so that education would grow from public interest and awareness, rather than be imposed from the top down.

Clean Harbors, Inc., met DEM's criteria, and its top management also agreed to meet with citizens' groups to learn from past siting experiences to shape a sound proposal. Alan McKim, the company's president, identified the Taunton Industrial Park as a good site. He met with Taunton's Mayor, Richard Johnson, who agreed to help McKim contact local public-interest groups and officials. He was willing to help ensure that the proposal would be given a fair hearing in Taunton.

Roger Hoffman is a cofounder and leader of the main community group in Taunton, the Whittenden Community Forum. Hoffman worked within the forum long before the Clean Harbors proposal, helping forum members to educate themselves on the issue of hazardous waste management. He noted, "It is much easier to be against a proposal than for one—because to be for one requires a great deal of research and education that goes well beyond that provided by government." Hoffman's group took a neutral stance on the proposal.

Both Mayor Johnson and Hoffman agreed that, with time, community acceptance of the facility could probably have been achieved. But before the proposal entered the formal review process, Clean Harbors decided to withdraw from Taunton. The strongest opposition finally came not from the community but from potential neighboring industries in the park, which were reluctant to enter into a purchase-and-sale agreement with the firm for fear of the effect of the facility on their businesses and on land values in the park.

Although the proposal never underwent Massachusetts' formal siting process, many lessons were learned about communicating risk, especially when dealing with perceived risk. The Taunton case is one in which communication played a significant role. Throughout the public meetings to shape the proposal, both the state (interested in ensuring the siting of a good facility to treat unmanaged wastes) and the developer (interested in moving forward on a project to meet significant specific demand) were intent on keeping lines of communication open. The credibility of the individuals involved was not in question.

The panel's discussion of the Taunton case revealed some interesting factors that diminish institutions' ability to overcome public fears and uncertainty about certain complex technologies, and that impede society's ability to cope with problems that can be alleviated by these technologies. First, the panelists noted that the public tends to trust individuals and institutions that do not necessarily have the most or best information on an issue, rather than those who are most likely to have such information: government and industry. Government, in particular, suffers from a loss of credibility; it is often perceived to have a hidden agenda rather than to facilitate a process. In a community, an individual clergyman, doctor, nurse, or lawyer is more likely to be heard than is a representative of government or an institution. One among many reasons for this credibility loss may rest in an institutional reluctance to deal forthrightly with *perceived* risks. This unwillingness results in anger, frustration, and finally a breakdown in communication.

Second, a major frustration for government representatives seeking solutions to particular problems lies in the difficulty of asking a local community to serve regional or even national needs. In this context, the panelists believed that the communication process is not something that can begin or end with a specific siting proposal. It is a long-term process. Institutions concerned with society's welfare must constantly appraise the need for technological solutions, keep abreast of developments in technologies with respect to their suitability and safety, and share this information with the public and special-interest groups. Beyond this, the panelists identified the need to analyze existing local risks when siting is foreseen in order to address these in the context of negotiations. There may be ways to derive direct benefits from the siting of a facility—benefits that will actually reduce health and environmental risks in the community.

Third, the panelists felt that compensation is one of the thorniest areas of communication with respect to siting technologies perceived to be high risk. Compensation is likely to be regarded as a bribe rather than an incentive at the local level. Cost/benefit analyses must be thorough and specific before any discussion of compensation will be meaningful, so that the community can weigh the perceived risk in the context of other community risks that must be mitigated if the perceived risk is assumed.

Finally, the Taunton experience makes clear that no matter how good or how long the communication process is, the local community must have *information* to participate effectively in the negotiation process. In this context, communicators must be clear in their own minds that the process is one of negotiation rather than manipulation. This point, panelists stressed, cannot be made strongly enough. Candor and honesty are essential ingredients in this process. Communicators must view the process as one of communicating the nature of the risk, rather than as one of manipulating the public into accepting a decision that has already been made.

Nuclear and Other Energy Sources

Panel Chairperson:
Robert C. Mitchell
Senior Fellow, Resources for the Future

Over the past 10 years, the nuclear energy conflict has provided both the main inspiration for the development of risk assessment and the greatest challenge to risk communication. As was made clear in this case study of nuclear energy, the problems surrounding the nuclear debate have not yet been resolved, but we now understand a great deal about their nature. The panel and the audience represented a microcosm of the conflict as it unfolded 5 to 10 years ago; two panel members were affiliated with pro- and antinuclear organizations, an equal number were journalists, and one was an academic observer. Not only was there great disagreement among the panelists, but audience participation indicated that positions have changed and passions cooled very little over the years. The risks presented by nuclear energy in the United States remain controversial, and this brings attendant difficulties in communicating them.

Panelists and members of the audience agreed that nuclear energy poses a somewhat different kind of risk problem than those discussed by other panels. The number of years during which nuclear energy has been controversial, the economic and political interests that have been involved, the extensive organizing that has taken place on both sides, and the social scale of the decisions under question have meant that attitudes toward this particular technological risk have been associated with a host of values and beliefs. Perhaps the key value questions that determine attitudes toward nuclear energy are whether one favors large- or small-scale organization and the priority one gives to economic growth as a social goal. These value questions are especially important because we have no personal experience, no "experiential handle" in Paul Slovic's words, with assessing the risks of nuclear energy. To form an opinion on nuclear energy involves a certain leap of imagination, and the only grounds for making this leap are our values and beliefs about how the world works.

The degree to which the nuclear issue is embedded in value systems and political debate makes it an extreme case for risk communicators, in the sense that any attempts to communicate technical information must take account of existing individual frameworks for interpreting that information. People do not receive information in a vacuum but rather try to make it compatible with other things they know about the world. They already know many things about nuclear energy, so that a lot of interpretation of new information takes place. (Compare nuclear energy with EDB: few members of the public had even heard of this pesticide, much less formed an opinion about it.)

The first implication of this public interpretation of technical information is that comparing different risks is difficult. One panelist remarked that the risks of nuclear energy are simply not comparable to the risks of eating too much salt. The reason for this is that the relevant trade-offs are different in the two cases. For nuclear energy, we must compare the risks of accidents and radiation with the hazards of coal-fired electricity or perhaps with the chance of reduced economic prosperity. In the case of eating salt, we think about how food tastes or our options for dining out. These are different realms of decision making, and the information that should be provided for each is different.

In fact, several panelists and members of the audience felt that nuclear energy is such a highly charged symbol that thinking in terms of risk is not the right way to view the conflict at all. It is perhaps more a question of a technological choice in the context of a highly political debate. This is certainly true of many foreign countries, where nuclear programs are more closely associated with the government than they are here. Attacking nuclear energy becomes a way to attack the government.

The fact that technical information is always filtered through political ideology also suggests that the nuclear issue is perhaps more a problem of ineradicable political differences than of bad communication from the experts to the public. (The strong feelings displayed during the panel discussion seem to support this.) The solution would be quite different for each problem. If the problem is that the public does not understand the technical information about risk that the "experts" are providing, and if there is reason to believe that citizens would accept this information if they understood it, the "message," "source," and "channel" problems are foremost. But if the public is not going to accept the arguments of the experts no matter how well they understand them, then it becomes most important to understand the "receivers" of the message and why they hold the positions they do.

The original inclination of experts when large numbers of the public did not accept their reassurances about nuclear energy was to regard the public as irrational. The precise risk figures calculated by the experts could not be questioned, so the public was instead. More recently, some observers have argued that the experts have been unreasonable in their focus on specific numbers and rates, especially fatality rates, and that the public has had a broader awareness of the effects of technology, one that takes into account a variety of sociological effects—a position consistent with the study by Covello, von Winterfeldt, and Slovic on risk communication [see the Appendix].

When there is still intense disagreement over a technology even after the facts are on the table, better risk communication is not the answer. Several panelists agreed that the best approach is to set up an effective political process for bargaining among the different sides. At the very least this involves letting each side articulate its position, respond to criticisms from the opposition, and have access to all relevant data. Trying to suppress one position will only force it into less rational channels. At this point there are two paths the political process could take. One is the "town meeting" model, in which everyone is given a chance to speak his or her piece and to convince others, after which a vote is taken. This model, which appears in the study just mentioned, implies that communication is crucial. An alternative is what seems to have happened in the nuclear debate: permanent organizations express the views of different segments of the public. Instead of having to learn about each issue separately and to form an opinion on each one, every citizen can find one or more organizations that represent his or her views on the issue fairly well. This alternative is more realistic in a complex society and follows the principle of representative government. Bargaining and communication among these organizations becomes an important challenge apart from that of how experts communicate risks to the public.

To show further that bad communication is not the major problem in the nuclear conflict, there was widespread agreement that "channel" problems are relatively few in this conflict. Many participants in the panel discussion agreed that the media actually do a fairly good job of reporting the facts that are given to them. The media seem to play a much greater role in simply defining an issue as important than in influencing what the public thinks about that issue.

More important than "channel" problems in the nuclear energy conflict are "source" problems. According to some panelists, the Nuclear Regulatory Commission (NRC) should have played a greater role as a source of neutral and objective information about nuclear energy and about what was happening in situations such as the Three Mile Island accident. Through occasional distortions and denials, the NRC lost a great deal of its credibility, not only with the antinuclear public but with the public at large. There was wide agreement on the panel that any lapses from the strict truth, even when that truth is simply that the experts don't know something, is deadly to an organization's credibility. And once that credibility is gone, it is very hard to regain.

Some present believed that the public doesn't expect a group to tell *the* truth, but only to tell *a* truth. By knowing the position and interests of the group, the public then knows how to situate the information provided. The problem with the NRC is that it has fudged its position, sometimes acting as regulator, sometimes taking the side of the utilities, sometimes acting as a general promoter of nuclear energy. Experts are often unwilling to admit that there is not one single truth, but once this is admitted it is easy to see the importance of knowing which truth someone is putting forward.

The public is familiar with politics; it is accustomed to receiving information embedded in arguments for certain policy positions. In fact, it is *not* used to receiving information in the abstract, ungrounded in some plea for action. So the communication of risk from experts to the public is not a simple matter: the links between the two are political organizations and ideologies. Information will be filtered through these in any case, so perhaps it should be placed in policy contexts from the start. "Receiver" problems consist not of finding out why the public is irrational, but of finding out what political positions have been staked out and how they relate to one another. Policy arguments are not a category that fits easily into the model of risk communications provided by Covello and his co-authors [see the Appendix].

To summarize this case study in terms of the four kinds of communication problems that Covello and his co-authors describe, channel problems turned out to be less important with regard to nuclear power than one might think; messages are interpreted according to the values and political positions of the receivers; and sources can be problematic when they attempt to step outside political positions or policy roles. Information to be communicated must fit into the frameworks of the receivers: because they will interpret the information according to these frameworks, we must be aware of what they are rather than bemoan their existence. The nuclear debate shows how important and irreducible receivers are.

EDB (Ethylene Dibromide)

Panel Chairperson:
Reed Johnson
Associate Professor of Economics, U.S. Naval Academy

There was clear agreement among the panelists discussing this case study that the EDB crisis may have been a perceptual or a regulatory crisis, but not a public health crisis. It was in fact a crisis of communication.

The message that U.S. Environmental Protection Agency (EPA) regulators tried to convey was that the food contamination risk from EDB was a long-term, rather than a short-term, risk. They were frustrated that they could not induce the media to accept and disseminate that message. Instead, public perception was dominated by images of squad cars rushing, their sirens wailing, to remove contaminated muffin mixes from supermarket shelves, and of EDB-chemical workers being carried off to hospitals to die.

The media transformed the EDB incident from a local regulatory issue into a national crisis. One participant in the discussion suggested that the media had been "hoodwinked" into treating EDB as a real public health crisis. Another argued that the media simply held up a mirror to our inability to cope with this particular problem. Still another emphasized the difference between macro and micro risks. Our regulatory institutions are designed to deal with scientific risk assessments that cast risk in terms of the probabilities of adverse health effects as a result of national population exposures. What ordinary citizens want and need to know is this: what is it safe to do in my own life?

The EDB communication problem was complicated by a number of factors, some of which were largely beyond the control of the EPA. Several panelists pointed out that the EPA had recently experienced a major crisis of leadership and was suffering from a general lack of confidence in its ability to deal effectively with environmental hazards. There was, moreover, a serious delay in the EPA's response to the initial discovery of food contamination in Florida. And the agency was bound by certain legal and regulatory procedures that hampered its ability to deal with the problem in an effective and timely way.

The Ruckelshaus news conference on EDB was the dramatic climax of the crisis. This news conference was staged as a deliberate and conscious attempt to inform and educate the public about the risks of EDB. It appears to have been a failure as an educational effort, but it was ultimately successful in laying the crisis to rest.

The news conference succeeded for two reasons. First, Mr. Ruckelshaus was able to inspire sufficient trust to restore public confidence in the EPA's competence to cope with the problem. Second, he delivered a concrete message: the action that was taken was appropriate and effective. Both these elements were probably necessary. Mr. Ruckelshaus could not have restored confidence without a message that people could believe and accept; similarly, Anne Burford could not have credibly conveyed the same message.

Although the panel did not explore how one might inspire confidence, the EDB incident is a good case study in the power of honesty and consistency. Mr. Ruckelshaus had the courage to say simply, "I don't know all the answers, but I am dealing with this problem as responsibly as I can." People believed him.

The panel was unable to resolve one important but troublesome issue. The public appears to suffer from a kind of schizophrenia with respect to risk. Our regulatory process is designed primarily to set safety standards and enforce them. The presumption behind these standards is that we can tell people that exposures below some critical level are safe. There seems to be an enormous public repository of faith in this approach most of the time. But sometimes, as in the case of EDB, this faith collapses and people are unwilling to accept, without considerable justification, official reassurances that the world is safe.

In that kind of situation, the macro risk orientation collides with the micro risk concerns of ordinary people. Because people are unwilling to accept the established standard, they demand to know the implications of what officials know so that they can make their own decisions. We do not seem to be as good at helping people make their own decisions as we are in making decisions for them by way of the standard-setting process.

Did we learn anything from the EDB incident? We might conclude from the fact that we have not had any similar crises in the last two years that we must have learned something. We can obtain some comfort in the fact that Alar,* for example, has not materialized into a nationwide crisis. However, we are confronting something that may be much more destructive than EDB, both in terms of public health and risk communication: radon.

At the EPA, concerns are being expressed that we are repeating some of our EDB-related mistakes: treating radon as a conventional standard-setting problem, failing to translate aggregate risk information into terms relevant for individual decision making, and allowing unconscionable delays that undermine public confidence. Perhaps the single most important lesson we should have learned from EDB is that waiting to gather more data and to jump through all the possible bureaucratic hoops can be fatal to the public confidence necessary for effective risk communication. In short: he or she who hesitates is lost.

---

*Editor's note: Alar is a pesticide widely used on fruit trees.

Panel

Future Challenges for Risk Communicators

Frederick W. Allen, Chairperson
Associate Director, Office of Policy Analysis, U.S. Environmental Protection Agency (EPA)

The four people on this panel will each speak briefly on the subject of future challenges for risk communicators. Then I am going to open it up for the audience to question the speakers and make other comments. I have asked the speakers to look at some of the more forward-oriented activities that they are involved in personally, and to reflect on some of the challenges that they see ahead not only for themselves but for others. I would like to pursue these issues in the discussion period.

I would also like to pose a question to everybody here in anticipation of the discussion period. From this conference we have momentum on an issue, an area of concern to us all. I would like to have more ideas, in the discussion that follows this panel or later, on what you think somebody—not necessarily the sponsors of this conference, but somebody—ought to be trying to do to meet these challenges.

Our first speaker is Alan McGowan, who is president of the Scientists' Institute for Public Information. I have asked him to describe his organization's work and then branch out from there.

Alan McGowan
President, Scientists' Institute for Public Information

Scientists' Institute for Public Information, the organization I direct, operates the Media Resource Service. It was started during the Three Mile Island incident, and it has gained some visibility since that time. It is a referral service for journalists working on stories having to do with science and technology. A journalist calls us, and we go to our files of more than 20,000 experts. We identify appropriate experts, call them when there is enough time in advance, alert them that a journalist will be calling, ask their permission for this, find out if they really are appropriate for the particular story, and—if they are not—try to find out who is. We then call the journalist back. We give him or her the names, backgrounds, and credentials of the experts to whom we are referring him or her. We also give the journalist some sense of where the experts are coming from on the particular issue; if it is controversial, we try to provide experts on both sides, to make sure that people talk from hard data, and so on. During the Bhopal incident, we received literally hundreds of calls. We have received even more than that in the past few days from journalists trying to find out about the space shuttle tragedy.

Let me give you a few examples of the kinds of calls we receive. Over 25 percent of the calls we get, and we are now averaging something like 60 to 70 calls a week from journalists around the country, are related to toxic substances, hazardous waste, chemicals, and so forth. Most of the concerns of these callers are health related: how dangerous is a substance, how safe is it, and so on. Over half of the calls have a local angle or are prompted by some emergency.

The journalist often calls under a deadline—sometimes 15 minutes—and says, "I need somebody right now, we have a radio program, a television program, and I have to find somebody immediately." This is one of the reasons why risk communicators must listen to and know their audience. In this case, the audience is the media. The media are often the translators and communicators of information from experts to the general public, and it is very important to pay attention to them.

Although we are staffed from early in the morning until late at night, something like 80 percent of all calls come in after 2:00 p.m. Most of them have to be answered that day. Recently, a call came in at

4:50 p.m. from the *Times Standard* of Eureka, California. Large quantities of chlorine gas are stored in that town for use in two paper pulp operations, and someone had questioned the possible health hazards of a leak or explosion. (We receive a large number of such "what if" calls.) In this case, we referred the journalist to Dan Mangel of Duke University Medical Center and Robert Faelin, who directs the Air Pollution Health Effects Laboratory at the University of California, Irvine. The headline that resulted was "Chlorine Can Be Dangerous, But Not Worst of Chemicals." The reporter stated that chlorine gas can cause harmful health effects and even death, depending upon how much and for how long chlorine is inhaled. Mr. Faelin commented that the journalist "asked good initial questions, listened patiently, and asked additional questions. The article was informative and had a realistic tone and perspective."

Another call came in recently from the Cuma, Louisiana, *Daily Courier*. The reporter stated that a Seattle-based company planned to install a PCB storage plant nearby and wanted to know the health hazards of PCB disposal. We referred him to Kevin Chisam of Versar, Inc.; John Cradick of Monsanto; Raymond Haborson of the University of Arkansas; and Shane Quihee of the University of Cincinnati Medical Center. The article's headline was "PCB's—How Dangerous Are They?" The scientists to whom the reporter was referred commented that his article was "better than average." I'm not quite sure what that means, given what some scientists feel about the average level of media reporting. Mr. Chisam felt that the particular subject is frequently sensationalized, but that this time it was reported objectively and clearly.

For another article in a magazine called *Science World*, for junior-high students, a reporter asked to speak to experts on the health hazards and regulatory history of asbestos. In this case, we referred the journalist to Al Alm, whom you have heard here; Irving Selikoff of Mount Sinai Hospital, New York; Tiber Asulata of the University of Minnesota; and Jim Merchant of the University of Iowa. The resulting article was headlined "Asbestos in the Classroom" and the lead was as follows: "According to a recent EPA report, over half of our nation's schools have failed to report whether or not they have an asbestos problem. Why are they receiving failing grades?" It went on to describe some of the problems, difficulties, and health hazards of asbestos. Al Alm felt that the article provided good background data on both the scientific aspects of asbestos contamination and government actions to cope with it. Irving Selikoff felt that it provided an excellent translation of complex scientific data without condescension.

What are some of the lessons that can be learned from these experiences? First, because in each case we called the scientists before the journalist called, they were prepared for the call, which I think is one of the most important lessons that we can learn. The second lesson concerns preparedness. During the Three Mile Island incident, ABC called me and said, "We need somebody to describe what is going on in that reactor." They said they would prepare a chart. The newscast team came into my living room on a Sunday morning, and their chart was almost completely wrong. It had almost everything backward. I do not know where they got the information, but they were going to show this chart on television. So we took out some crayons and cardboard and we manufactured something better. This is not exactly what I call being prepared! But it *is* possible to be prepared, and it is possible to be prepared without visuals. Television, as we all know, wants visuals. And in a crisis such as Bhopal, Three Mile Island, or the *Challenger*, television accounts for about 80 percent of our calls. It wants information, right away.

Most people will absorb the most information during a crisis. If you talk about risk assessment when there is a crisis, people are really interested. We learned more, unfortunately, about the *Challenger* and its operations on Tuesday night than we have learned about space flights during the many years of the space program.

Accidents are going to occur. Maybe simply a local spill, a rather small one—but some accidents are going to occur. We must learn to move quickly and to not dodge, fudge, avoid, or run away. Risk communicators must be responsive to the journalists' needs. I am talking about journalists here, about communicating with the public through the media. We should let experts talk to the media; we should not shield experts with public information people. Public information directors can play a crucial role, but experts should be asked to talk even if they might tell a slightly different story. They are, after all, the ones who may know what is going on.

It is important to know the media before a crisis erupts. The time to be introduced to somebody who is going to write a story on a particular incident is not when it occurs. Take a journalist to lunch, get to know him or her, and communication can be a lot more effective.

Perhaps the most important thing is to be honest. We need to say we do not know if we don't, not try to make something up.

These guidelines sound simple, but in the words of Covello and his co-authors, they are continually and consistently violated. It takes work to adhere to them. It takes planning, and it takes being prepared.

Claudine Schneider
U.S. House of Representatives

I would like to share with you some of what I see as our priorities, although some of the points I will make have been made by previous speakers. Perhaps my contribution to this conference will come through the question-and-answer period, where I can explain how I take on the responsibility of being a "representative of the people." As a result of the rapid development of new technologies and new products, which for the most part have enhanced our quality of life, we are confronted with a whole series of new challenges that bring with them certain problems. One of the best examples of this situation is the energy crisis of the 1970s. New energy-conserving technologies did develop as a result of this crisis: we found new ways to build more energy-efficient homes and workplaces. That has improved our quality of life, decreased our energy consumption and energy costs, and stabilized to a degree our energy supply. Yet we are now recognizing a new challenge, a new problem—indoor air pollution.

Many of you may not know much about indoor air pollution, and you might think that it is something we should not be concerned with. However, some studies have estimated that the problem of indoor air pollution could be anywhere from 10 to 100 times worse than any other environmental hazard that we now have to deal with. (I will focus specifically on the problem of radon in our indoor environment, later on.)

There is a role for energy, industry, and the private sector in this and other new challenges. As previous speakers have mentioned, the only way that we can successfully go about communicating the potential risks associated with these challenges is by forming coalitions or making partnership arrangements.

There is a group in the Boston area, called Common Ground, whose purpose is to assemble coalitions of different interests—government, industry, or the private sector—to tackle environmental problems. Common Ground works by "networking" information among various decision makers and researchers and then communicating that information to the general public. It is a good model, I think, for the kind of partnerships we now need.

We have to begin with basic philosophical questions: What is the public's right to know? How much does the government let the public know? What is our responsibility as government policy makers or researchers or industry managers? We all have a duty as decision makers to reveal enough information so that we can at least hint at potential health and safety threats. The challenge in communicating potential risks to the public is primarily to establish credibility. It is very difficult to establish credibility unless you have facts. And when we are talking about risks, we are talking about scientific data. Some science underlies any information on risk that is in a meaningful sense credible.

Returning to the issue of indoor air pollution, we know that there are 120,000 cases of lung cancers each year, and that anywhere from 12,000 to 20,000 of those lung cancers are believed to be attributable to sources of indoor air pollution. Radon, a naturally occurring radioactive gas, is believed to be one of the major contributing sources. Unlike other forms of pollution, indoor air pollution does not belch out as black smoke from smoke stacks; it does not cause dead fish to float on the surface of the water. It is no less lethal for this, however. What we have to realize is that we have the potential for a major crisis here, and we know that from the limited scientific data that has been accumulated by the Environmental Protection Agency (EPA), by the Consumer Product Safety Commission, and the Department of Energy.

I would like to share with you the process, and some of the problems, of communicating the risks of indoor air pollution. Within Congress, the first need was for scientific data; thus, in the budgetary process, I suggested that we fund research on three things: the sources of indoor air pollution, the connection (if any) between these sources and human health, and any measures that could be taken—by industry or the consumer—to mitigate the potential problems. Fortunately, Congress now has funding to do the research needed before we can communicate whether there are risks associated with indoor air pollution.

But we are facing a special problem right now in the area of research—in providing adequate scientific data on which policy makers can base sound decisions. When we look at the amount of resources that the federal government has committed to defining the extent of particular environmental problems, we find that we are losing our information base. The gap between spending on defense research and civilian research continues to widen, and it will intensify the task of communicating whatever accurate information we do have on the kinds of risks the public may be exposed to.

We need strong scientific data on which to base our policies and regulations; we also need it so we can avoid court battles. Those here who represent industry and the EPA can attest to the fact that we waste millions of dollars and vast amounts of time on the various court battles that we have been involved in—and threats to public health continue.

As we consider the process of communicating risks involved in a particular product or technology, we have to keep in mind that the people who will be receiving this information will in turn consider its source. This is where coalitions become important. There have been a number of polls on public perceptions of credibility. In one, environmentalists had the highest credibility; consumer groups were at the top of the list, and industry and labor unions were at the bottom. At the very bottom were government officials.

As an elected official, I find it necessary to build and maintain credibility, and one of the most effective ways to do that is through coalition building. Here is a concrete example. I had introduced a proposal called the waste-end tax, which is a funding mechanism for Superfund that would encourage the recycling and reuse of hazardous waste. After putting together the draft legislation, I gave a copy to members of the environmental community and the Chemical Manufacturers' Association. They both reviewed the draft, which became as a result an equitable piece of legislation. This partnering of two opposing groups helped not only my credibility but also the passage of the legislation. Although as the debate continued, we lost some of the support of each group, we did succeed in passing the bill in the House. The strategy of building credibility through coalitions is one that more often than not is successful.

The other issue we have to keep in mind is that of the quality of the information we seek to communicate. Information should be timely, and even if it is inconclusive, it must be shared with the public. Another specific example that immediately comes to mind in this regard is acid rain. We *know* that acid rain is a problem. Yet, regrettably, the [Reagan] administration has chosen not to recommend any policy changes but rather to spend more money on research. We could forestall some of the damage that is occurring and that will continue to occur by beginning to take some actions even though our information is not 100 percent conclusive—as we have done, for instance, with cigarette smoking. The fact that warning labels on cigarette packages state that cigarette smoking may be hazardous to our health is a responsible move. If someone tells me that something *may* be dangerous, then I am going to give them the benefit of the doubt.

As risk communicators, we have a responsibility to draw fine lines, to determine how much scientific data we really need before we divulge what we know or suspect about a particular activity or condition. It is critically important to emphasize diagnostic and preventive measures.

What we need is a well-defined process for divulging information. Managers need to have a procedure that they follow, one that will more often than not have as its focus preventive measures. Individuals are looking for the opportunity to feel empowered, and it is our opportunity to make sure that they do not feel helpless when they do receive information.

As a policy maker, I have to ask questions of those who are generating information, but I also have to answer to my constituents and to the public at large. To do so, I must have accurate information presented in a credible way. I would like to share with you what kind of help I need. First and foremost, I need your assistance in heightening public awareness as to the value of the federal government's investing more dollars and energy in basic research and basic information gathering. Industry as well as government has to stress the importance of the federal research budget for the public good.

I hope that you will join me in working to improve the credibility of policy makers, government officials, and industry representatives. The challenge that we face is not just deciding what to communicate. It is a challenge not just of content but also of style. As we put our heads together, we ought to be able to come up with appropriate formulas for building credibility across the board—and this should help us to minimize the number of risks that the public is exposed to.

Jackson Browning
Vice-President for Health, Safety, and Environmental Affairs, Union Carbide Corporation

It is appropriate that we are having this discussion about risk communication in a hotel. Years ago it was rare to see maps in hotels describing emergency escape routes; even mentioning the possibility of fire was taboo. The assumption was that talk of emergencies would only scare people away. Today these maps, along with other information, are in plain view—and they make people feel more secure, not less.

Like the hotel industry, the chemical industry is living in this new era. We are communicating more to the people in the communities around our plants about the nature of what we do and the hazards that are certainly involved. And they are communicating to us their concerns and their needs for information. With the hotel industry, the fear of such communication was canceled bookings; our challenge is to openly communicate risks and our continuing efforts to reduce them without thereby canceling our industry. I think we can do this—but we could use some help.

Increasing communication should make our communities safer. But risk communicators have a responsibility to make sure not only that they have the facts but also that they can help people understand what the facts mean. We can fulfill our responsibilities as risk communicators only by becoming partners, not competitors, in that process.

Today I would like to explore the question of keeping risk in perspective. Fear can be a healthy response when the danger is real and when fear prompts us to proper action. But at least in relation to chemical technology, fear is often of the irrational, phobic variety. It is often the outcome of information that is inaccurate, exaggerated, or presented in a way that is calculated to alarm.

Every chemical company has its favorite examples of this. I can illustrate the point with some of the media accounts of events at our plant in Institute, West Virginia. The first of these reports concerned an accidental release of reaction products from a tank containing aldicarb oxime and other chemicals during the summer of 1985, not too long after the incident in Bhopal.

Twenty-eight people were hospitalized overnight, but in the news stories that followed the event, this figure was multiplied by nearly five to 135. Now, the media didn't pull this figure out of thin air. In fact, 135 people checked into hospitals, but only 28 were actually admitted. Nevertheless, 135 remains the number of people cited in many of the stories referring to that event.

The figure is not a harmless mistake such as misreporting a company's promotion or retirement policy. The media took an incident that was not life threatening and, in misreporting it, caused people to believe that an entire community might have been at risk—and the fact that a Union Carbide plant was involved helped to make it news across the country.

Here is a second incident involving misreported figures. In January 1984, before the Bhopal incident, we had a spill at Institute involving 5 pounds of liquid methyl isocyanate, which is the same material that was released in Bhopal as a gas. A year after the release, the 5-pound release was reported as having been 840 pounds. (This is when people were digging into the history of the Institute plant after the 5-pound release.) In fact, the spill was quickly neutralized within the plant with equipment designed and provided for that purpose. It was so minor as to present no danger to the community involved and did not require reporting at that time to the EPA.

But what if you had heard about a spill of 840 pounds of this substance, which had not been previously reported in the media? Your reaction might be very strong. Coming so soon after Bhopal, the national reaction was indeed strong. After we had a chance to sift through the data, we found that the 840-pound figure had indeed come from company documents supplied to the EPA. We also discovered that the figure was an extrapolation, not an actual measurement, and was based on a mistaken assumption about the source tank for the material involved. True, a quick glance at the report might have led you to think that 840 pounds was the actual amount, but a check with Union Carbide would have revealed that the correct number was 5 pounds.

On an issue so sensitive, not just for us but for the whole community, it may seem too much to expect a reporter to do some careful checking. I understand the pressures to be first in print or on the air; but particularly where the community welfare is involved, being right should be more important than being first. It seems that when chemical operations are involved, misinformation has a life of its own.

In December 1984, reporters had the idea that we had computerized safety operations at Institute, while safety at the Bhopal plant was left to the operators. And to this day, stories repeat the erroneous notion that computerized safety devices were in place at Institute but were not in place at Bhopal. Who is to blame?

The time has come for me to cast the first stones, and you may be surprised at the direction in which I cast them. I place a lot of the blame for these and similar communication failures on the scarcity of company managers at the local level who are adequately equipped to serve as risk communicators. The second stone is for the media. Reporters are also risk communicators. Seeing that the public is well and carefully informed about risk is a shared responsibility that should fall on the company and the media alike. The less we see risk communication as a partnership, the more we are likely to see harmful inaccuracies. Conversely, the more fully we work together at communicating the facts, the more credible we will all be, and the better the public will be served.

At this point, I would like to suggest some challenges for risk communicators addressing each side of the community/media equation. As to the community side, chemical companies must equip plant managers so that they can handle community relations effectively. Union Carbide has greatly heightened its attention to this process by holding regional seminars for plant managers on community and media relations. Our managers must be able to think clearly in an emergency situation, whether it is handling a mechanical problem in the plant, a controversial topic raised by the media, or an emotionally charged confrontation with members of the community. Managers need to be able to assess a situation quickly, get the facts, and communicate them clearly to the community and the media, even when everyone around them is shouting accusations.

Companies must also produce materials that communicate the nature of the risks in terms that people in the community can understand. Some of the materials available in the past (we called them material safety data sheets) contained highly technical information often written by technical people and for a mostly technical audience. Consequently, the challenge here is to provide complete yet understandable information and to make that information easily accessible to the public.

This work is going forward throughout the industry. We need materials that provide practical information on what the public should do in an emergency situation involving chemicals. Union Carbide, for example, in close consultation with local safety and emergency-response officials and community representatives, helped develop integrated community emergency-response plans for the communities near its Institute and South Charleston, West Virginia, plants. We then underwrote brochures that outline specific procedures that residents near the plants could follow in an emergency. Every household in these communities has been given such a brochure.

In another example, the EPA has recommended that information regarding the possible health hazards of about 400 chemicals be given wide distribution to the local health and safety officials. Union Carbide deals with less than 30 percent of those chemicals, and most of our operating locales deal with only a very few, if any. We have already supplied the communities at all our major locations with information on these materials, and we are moving forward as quickly as possible to provide it to every location.

There are, to be sure, some problems with the list. One of the materials that is listed, for example, is nicotine. It is of course highly toxic, but the real risk is in the puff, not the tank load. It is important to know the risks out there; it is even more important to know which ones to worry about.

Now we should look at the media side of the equation. The first challenge is to understand that environmental reporting is serious business: once people are scared, they tend to stay scared. The second challenge is to encourage reporters to refrain from creating a story to suit program or editorial needs. (Here is an example of this. I once attended a seminar on behalf of the Chemical Manufacturers' Association. The seminar happened to take place not far from a newly discovered toxic dump site. A reporter asked me if I knew about the site, and I replied that I did not. Later I was surprised to find a picture of myself on the local news, cleverly juxtaposed with footage of the site; the clear implication was that I was investigating the dump site in my capacity as a Chemical Manufacturers' Association representative. Facts were knowingly distorted to convey an impression about the site and its dangers that matched the station's concerns and story line.)

The third challenge is more subtle: to be not only guided but indeed disciplined by the facts, even when this means voluntarily underreporting when you do not have all the information and toning down the rhetoric to match the facts. In short, it is time for the media to calm the debate and get back to the facts.

A magazine showing an artist's fanciful rendition of a man sinking into a cesspool and losing his skin on the way down does not serve the public well. It is easy to understand that reporters want their stories to be as close to the front page or the beginning of the newscast as possible; reporters have a vested interest in catastrophies, and they seem to find them with ease when chemicals are involved. However, the role of the reporter should be comparable to that of the person assigned to inform people in a theater of a fire. That person becomes a risk communicator with all the responsibility that the phrase should imply. If he fails to inform people of the danger, he fails in his role. If he goes into the theater and frightens people by screaming at the top of his lungs, he also fails in his role. The objective should be to achieve an orderly withdrawal from the fire and the method must suit the situation. Excited, sensational reporting has no place in this situation or in any other where people's safety and welfare is concerned.

Those of us in chemical companies can err by saying too little, and those in the media by saying too much. All of us can err by not double-checking our facts. Like those who work for chemical companies, journalists face the challenge of keeping information about risks in perspective. We must both accept that our goal is to keep improving as risk communicators.

Lewis Crampton
Executive Director, National Institute for Chemical Studies

I would like to first provide some background on how and why the National Institute for Chemical Studies was created, and then to present a brief outline of how the institute is facilitating the process of gathering concerned parties to sort through the risks, benefits, and choices that confront people living as close neighbors with major elements of the chemical processing industry in West Virginia's Kanawha Valley. Having done that, I want to offer a brief paradigm for risk communication, which will show how it works in theory and practice. Finally, I would like to provide some examples of how we are beginning to develop a problem-solving dialogue among the public, the chemical industry, public officials, and the media in the Kanawha Valley. I'm not holding out our experience as a model for every situation, of course; but I do think that useful insights can be gained from it.

The National Institute for Chemical Studies was formed in the wake of Bhopal. We were set up to serve as a bridge between the public and the chemical industry, which accounts for over 10 percent of the manufacturing jobs in the Kanawha Valley, West Virginia. This valley is located along a 35-mile stretch of the Kanawha River; its epicenter is Charleston, the state capital. Some 15 to 17 chemical processing plants are located there: Union Carbide has three facilities in the valley, and Monsanto, du Pont, FMC, Olin, and Diamond Shamrock all have significant operations there as well. West Virginia's Kanawha Valley happens to have one of the eight or nine largest concentrations of chemical processing facilities in the United States—and it is also highly visible, given the significant national publicity that surrounded the accidental release of aldicarb oxime by a Union Carbide facility here last August [in Institute, West Virginia].

The National Institute for Chemical Studies was founded by a group of local businesspeople, many of them fourth- and fifth-generation residents of Charleston. These people were worried about the negative perceptions they felt the rest of the country had of this area, and so they got together with Governor [Arch A.] Moore, Senator [Jay] Rockefeller, Senator [Robert C.] Byrd, and Congressman [Bob] Wise to create the institute as a means of altering these perceptions. At its inception, we tried to build a coalition that was representative of all groups in the valley, one that could stand alone as a credible source and communicator of information. Accordingly, we added to the institute's board the director of the state's leading environmental action group, the West Virginia Citizens Action Group; a toxicologist nominated by the West Virginia Lung Association; a human services program advocate who worked for the West Virginia Council of Churches; and two local college presidents. Thus, we created a board perceived by all parties as a credible entity, in a position to convene workshops and meetings, study problems, and help people to determine how effectively local chemical risks were being assessed and managed by local company managers and public officials.

The institute's financial support comes from the state of West Virginia; the Virginia Environmental Endowment; private subscriptions by local banks, businesses, and insurance companies in the Charleston metropolitan area; environmental foundations; federal grants; and support from du Pont, Monsanto, Union Carbide, and FMC. Initial guidance for the institute came from William D. Ruckelshaus, former administrator of the EPA, who currently serves as chair of the institute's National Advisory Board.

The institute has five broad goals. The first is to secure all requisite assurances from industry and local officials concerning protection of the public health, safety, and the environment. The second is to include the public directly in a process of identifying environmental or health risks and determining what is being done or should be done to eliminate, control, or minimize these risks. The third, consistent with the process described above, is to gain knowledgeable support of the general public for actions that can be taken to protect health and the environment. The fourth is to generate institutional and public support for preserving the economic base and benefits of the valley. And the fifth is to serve as a national model in the development of new approaches for citizens and the chemical industry to take in seeking solutions to some of the complex problems that arise from living and working with toxic and hazardous substances.

All of this was summarized in a few words by a famous early environmental planner, Rene Dubos, who said: "We should think globally and act locally." This advice guides the institute's approach. In the Kanawha Valley and everywhere in this country, the amount, quality, and degree of understanding about health, safety, and environmental issues involving the chemical processing industry are appallingly low. What has developed in the valley that is not yet taking place elsewhere is the negotiation of a real commitment from our major chemical companies to act out of a sense of stewardship relative to their local operations and to share with us important health, safety, and environmental information.

Why is this so important? Professionals in this field know that when it comes to getting the data needed to develop the most efficient and effective strategies to protect human health and the environment, the chemical companies are by far the best sources of this information. In the past, it has been difficult for these companies to acknowledge that it is in their best interest to make this information available as an act of corporate stewardship. But things are changing in the valley. Our companies are not only going beyond legal and regulatory requirements for sharing important information about health and safety factors, but they are even spending considerable sums to clean up their operations and safeguard against accidents well in advance of any regulatory or legal requirement to do so.

The National Institute for Chemical Studies is building a context for problem solving by using available information to develop mutual understanding between the industry and the public. In the valley, the chemical companies are willing to work with us because they view the Kanawha Valley as a kind of laboratory for trying out new ways of doing business. For example, we have encouraged a number of companies to work with the State Air Board to develop their own programs to voluntarily reduce air emissions and the amounts of hazardous materials used or stored on site. Last week the West Virginia Air Pollution Control Commission announced that four companies—Union Carbide, Monsanto, du Pont, and Diamond Shamrock—have agreed to cut their emissions of toxic air pollutants by over 2,500 tons per year. That is about 25 percent of total plantwide air emissions for the six largest facilities in the valley.

We have invited the Harvard School of Public Health to come to the valley to undertake a health effects exposure study. The chemical companies are cooperating by providing data. They are also participating in our Safeguards Program, in which we are merging key elements of the EPA's Chemical Emergency Preparedness Program with the Community Awareness and Emergency Response (CAER) program of the Chemical Manufacturers' Association to develop an inventory of high-hazard chemicals in the valley, map their location for the public, and then sponsor a public dialogue among chemical plant managers, first responders, and the public to determine how effectively accident-prevention and emergency-response programs are working. And, finally, we are also working with the EPA and the West Virginia Air Pollution Control Commission to develop a rough environmental "road map" of the valley based on emissions-modeling techniques developed by the EPA's Integrated Environmental Management Program. When completed, we will have a sense of which pollutants, concentration levels, sources, and geographic areas may be of potential concern as a long-term result of routine allowable emissions from local chemical plants.

With this as background, I would like to get back to the topic of risk communication. Certainly, having and using the kind of information I have just described to assess and manage potential risks is important. Indeed, it is quite clear that effective risk communication won't happen without good data. But what I want to share with you today concerns another of the institute's programs. It is related to finding the best way to process and work through all the available information so that we can empower people to use their understanding of an issue. I want to discuss the Dialogue Campaign, a conflict-resolution program we are just beginning in West Virginia; but before I do that, I will lay out the five theoretical principles upon which the dialogue and conflict resolution program is based.

First, the end product of the program is the development of a real sense of *public judgment* in the valley on such complex questions as whether negative health, safety, and environmental impacts of dangerous chemicals can be presumed to pre-exist. What we have now is public opinion. Public judgment will emerge as the end product of a long process of confrontation and resolution that proceeds on both the cognitive and the emotional level. Public judgment, which is what we expect to get after this process is completed, results when trivial risks are clearly separated from important risks, thereby giving the community a chance to focus its problem-solving efforts where they will do the most good.

Second, this working through of divergent opinions must happen under conditions that are free from domination and distortion and in a setting of impartiality and credibility—where no one point of view dominates or carries any special weight because of coercion, wealth, or media bias.

Third, the process of examining and coming to terms with complex issues must proceed by way of dialogue. No matter how well-intended, company monologues on their health, safety, and environmental programs are simply not effective. Kanawha Valley plant managers are now at the point where they are more than willing to talk—but this is still, from their standpoint, a process of talking *to* people, not *with* people. Now as never before, the companies are prepared to initiate a dialogue, but the community (even one as sophisticated as ours) lacks the capacity to involve itself in productive discussions on chemical health, safety, and environmental issues because people lack the information they need to ask the right questions. Communities such as ours need help in getting the required information into the public domain in a meaningful fashion so that productive dialogue can occur. That is the kind of service a coalition organization such as the National Institute for Chemical Studies is best equipped to provide.

Fourth, the required information has to undergo some preparatory analysis that separates out facts from values and then develops alternative choices around which various segments of public judgment can coalesce. This is necessary so we know what we are talking about. We need to have agreement on what the facts are and where they are in dispute, as well as an acknowledgment of the various points of view people are bringing to the process.

And, finally, a credible, honest broker or moderator is needed to encourage and manage this process. A local organization is usually best—one that respects people, listens well, and understands local ways of doing things. One obvious question that arises here is what kinds of institutions are best at sponsoring a dialogue on chemical health, safety, and environment issues. Some have said government might be the best local convener, but government even at the local level tends to lack the flexibility required for managing an effective dialogue on risks. Industry is willing to get involved, as the CAER program proves, but industry's main problem is that most people just aren't willing to trust chemical companies to present an objective analysis of the situation. There have been instances where court-appointed academics or professional mediators have been used with good results, but usually in such instances the major participants have been debating outcomes and alternatives for a long time.

Clearly, the best approach to developing consensus at the local level is to develop a coalition organization to process and present information on chemical risks. As our survey data conclusively show, coalition-based groups have credibility, which is a necessary precondition for managing any dialogue.

I will now turn to how the institute began to develop its Dialogue Campaign in the valley. After a series of focus-group interviews shortly after the well-publicized release of aldicarb oxime in West Virginia last August, the institute conducted a major public-opinion survey of people's attitudes toward the chemical industry and how they viewed the risks, benefits, and choices that are a constant part of living with the chemical industry in the Kanawha Valley.

We found, first, that there is a strong reservoir of general good will for the chemical companies in the valley. These companies are not looked upon as evil-doers. In fact, people in the valley are invested in their success to a considerable extent. Disturbingly, we also found that although people in the valley want both a sound economy and a healthy environment, they currently feel they have neither. They are depressed at the disparity between what they want and what they have, and they are not optimistic that conditions will improve in the near future. Interestingly enough, we learned that people are willing to make trade-offs to improve economic conditions, but only within limits and not generally at the risk of health or safety, or by rolling back environmental regulations. And, although we did find that people believe the chemical industry has helped improve the environment in the valley in recent years, they question the companies' commitment to further reducing health and environmental hazards. Moreover, it is clear that people do not entirely trust the companies as reliable sources of information about health, safety, or environmental conditions. As communicators on these issues, therefore, the chemical companies are laboring under a major credibility handicap.

We also found, surprisingly perhaps, that the public is not apathetic about getting involved. Local people want more information on chemical risks in their community, and they want the opportunity to register their concerns with public officials and with chemical plant managers. Finally, our survey indicated that although nobody is perceived as being supremely credible as a source of information and consensus-building around local safety, health, and environmental issues, a coalition of representatives of chemical companies, environmental groups, academic institutions, and state and local governments has the most potential to be perceived as a credible broker and source of knowledge for the general public.

What does all of this mean for the future of risk communication in communities such as ours? First, certain preconditions are needed for effective dialogue on risk to take place. For example, the fact that people do recognize that the industry confers real benefits on people is most important. In the valley no one is seriously advocating a zero-risk situation—what we are trying to achieve is some definition of a situation of acceptable risk that is achievable now with a reasonable amount of effort, so that we can chip away at remaining residual risks later.

Second, it is crucial that none of the participants in such a dialogue be made to feel that they are dealing from weakness. Although the benefits of the chemical industry are appreciated here in the valley, concerns about health, safety, and the environment have an even higher priority, according to our opinion surveys. The national media tend to view the Kanawha Valley in somewhat patronizing terms. To them, because West Virginia has such a high unemployment rate, its people have been forced to put up with bad air and dangerous conditions. This image of Kanawha Valley's citizens caught up in a Faustian bargain with the devil for jobs and industry is at odds with survey data showing strong local resistance to rolling back environmental standards, a desire for even stricter enforcement against violators, and a clearly stated preference for health, safety, and environmental benefits over employment benefits when people are forced to choose among them.

Three, we should accept that the public is interested, aware, and wants to be involved in environmental, health, and safety issues. The institute is not interested in developing a dialogue for its own sake. We are filling a need because most people in the valley recognize the existence of problems that could result in real disaster if they are not resolved. The Kanawha Valley needs, respects, and does not want to lose its chemical industry—but [the valley] won't be sacrificed to [the industry] either. Hence, we are developing our Dialogue Campaign to take people beyond a recognition of the fact that we have problems to the point where they are grappling with the hard choices that these problems present. This is why dialogue on risks, benefits, and choices is based on a crucial distinction between public opinion, which is a top-of-the-head reaction to an issue, and public judgment, which is how people feel about something after they have had a chance to think about it.

We are managing this dialogue process to help people separate trivial from important risks so that our collective problem-solving efforts can be focused on real issues with a minimum of distraction. The institute is serving as a neutral, nonpartisan overseer of the debate. We are creating a context for building understanding by procuring the information that is needed, giving people time to work through a problem, and providing a point in the process at which people can register collectively their judgment on the issues and choices that have been discussed during the Dialogue Campaign.

This process is expected to lead to a working consensus on actions that can be taken by local officials and industry to resolve some of these key issues. We will attempt to develop some degree of popular consensus on (1) measures or alternative actions that are readily acceptable to the public; (2) actions that have appeal, but about which all acknowledge that more information is needed before we can move forward; and (3) actions or alternatives that clearly are not acceptable or about which opinion is markedly divided.

This kind of effort is experimental and has not been attempted before with such volatile issues. Our closest antecedent is the dialogue on costs and benefits that occurred prior to the EPA's decision on regulatory alternatives in the Tacoma Smelter case. Ultimately, what we are trying to do is empower people to transform their perceptions about risks into knowledge and understanding. In the valley, we are learning that familiarity with the facts breeds not contempt but rather the ability to discriminate between slight and important risks. Fear is, after all, what has paralyzed policy with regard to these issues. And our experience thus far shows that familiar risks engender less fear than unfamiliar ones.

If we are not effective in communicating the risks of a technology such as chemical processing—which has been around now for over 60 years—then our capacity to maintain our leading edge in economic development and technological innovation is in doubt. The chemical industry's technologies, after all, are not the only ones that inspire fear and loathing on the part of many Americans. New developments in biotechnology and nuclear energy—and new, tough questions surrounding them—are on the horizon. Assessing, managing, and communicating chemical risks will better prepare us to cope with a future dominated by barely imaginable technologies and fraught with unfamiliar risks.

Appendix

Communicating Scientific Information about Health and Environmental Risks: Problems and Opportunities from a Social and Behavioral Perspective

Vincent T. Covello
National Science Foundation
Detlof von Winterfeldt
Institute of Safety and Systems Science, University of Southern California
Paul Slovic
Decision Research

Risk communication assumes a variety of forms, ranging from warning labels on consumer products to interactions among government officials, industry representatives, the media, and members of the public with regard to such highly charged locales and occurrences as Love Canal, EDB contamination of food, Three Mile Island, cigarette

---

*Note: This appendix is a revised version of a paper prepared as background for the National Conference on Risk Communication, Washington, D.C., January 1986.

smoking, asbestos in school buildings, and Chernobyl. Experience has shown that risk communication efforts are a source of frustration for both risk communicators and the intended recipients of the information. Government officials, industry representatives, and scientists note that laypeople frequently do not understand highly technical risk information and that individual biases and limitations may lead to distorted and inaccurate perceptions of many risk problems. Representatives of citizen groups and individual citizens are often equally frustrated, perceiving risk communicators and risk assessment experts to be uninterested in their concerns and unwilling to take immediate and direct actions to solve seemingly straightforward health, safety, and environmental problems. In this context, the media often play the role of transmitter and translator of information. But the media have been criticized for exaggerating or ignoring certain risks and for emphasizing drama over scientific facts.

A recent review of the literature (Covello, Slovic, and von Winterfeldt, 1986) on efforts to communicate information about health and environmental risk—such as the risks of saccharin, EDB, dioxin, AIDS, toxic waste, smoking, driving without seat belts, and nuclear power plant accidents—suggests that risk communication problems fall into four basic categories: (1) message problems resulting from limitations of scientific methods, analyses, and assessments; (2) source problems resulting from limitations of risk communicators and risk assessment experts; (3) channel problems resulting from limitations of the means by which scientific and technical information about health or environmental risks is transmitted; and (4) receiver problems stemming from certain characteristics of the intended recipients of the communication (see table 1).

Message problems include the following:
- deficiencies in scientific understanding, data, models, and methods, which result in large uncertainties in risk estimates; and
- highly technical analyses that are often unintelligible to laypersons.

Source problems include the following:
- lack of trust and credibility;
- disagreements among scientific experts;
- limited authority and resources for addressing risk problems;
- lack of data addressing the specific fears and concerns of individuals and communities;

Table 1
Problems in Risk Communication

Origin of the Problem	Example	Nature of the Problem
Message problems	Government or industry data on health risks	High level of scientific complexity Large data uncertainties
Source problems	Government or industry officials	Lack of institutional trust and credibility Expert disagreements Use of technical, bureaucratic language
Channel problems	Media	Selective and biased reporting Focus on sensational or dramatic aspects Premature disclosure of scientific information Inaccuracies and distortions
Receiver problems	Individual citizens	Inaccurate perceptions of risk Lack of interest Overconfidence in ability to avoid harm Unrealistic demands for scientific certainty Reluctance to make trade-offs

- failure to disclose limitations of risk assessments and resulting uncertainties;
- limited understanding of the interests, concerns, fears, values, priorities, and preferences of individual citizens and public groups; and
- use of bureaucratic, legalistic, and technical language.

Channel problems include the following:

- selective and biased media reporting that emphasizes drama, wrongdoing, disagreements, and conflict;
- premature disclosures of scientific information; and
- oversimplification and distortions of, as well as inaccuracies in, interpreting technical risk information.

Receiver problems include the following:

- inaccurate perceptions of levels of risk;
- lack of interest in risk problems and technical complexities;
- overconfidence in the ability to avoid harm;
- strong beliefs and opinions that are resistant to change;

- exaggerated expectations about the effectiveness of regulatory actions;
- desire and demand for scientific certainty;
- reluctance to make trade-offs among different types of risk or among risks, costs, and benefits; and
- difficulties in understanding probabilistic information related to unfamiliar technology.

Given these problems and the widespread dissatisfaction with the current state of risk communication, increasing numbers of researchers have turned their attention to the problems of risk communication. Much of their work has focused on communications between government agencies and the public. Such communications are currently the subject of intense controversy and represent one of the most challenging and difficult aspects of risk management today (Ruckelshaus, 1984; U.S. Environmental Protection Agency, 1984). Reflecting the broad scope of risk communication, the literature on this area encompasses such diverse fields as cognitive psychology, social psychology, consumer behavior, marketing, advertising, economics, mass communications, linguistics, anthropology, decision science, sociology, political science, health education, behavioral medicine, public health, environmental health, law, and philosophy.

RISK COMMUNICATION TASKS AND PROBLEMS

For purposes of this appendix, risk communication is defined as any purposeful exchange of information about health or environmental risks between interested parties. More specifically, risk communication is the act of conveying or transmitting information between interested parties about levels of health or environmental risks; the significance or meaning of such risks; or decisions, actions, or policies aimed at managing or controlling such risks. Interested parties include government agencies, corporations and industry groups, unions, the media, scientists, professional organizations, public-interest groups, and individual citizens.

As shown in table 2, risk communication tasks can be organized into four general types, according to the primary objective or intended effect of the communication:

1. information and education;
2. behavior change and protective action;

Table 2
A Typology of Risk Communication Objectives

Type 1: Information and Education
> Informing and educating people about risks and risk assessment in general.
> Example: Statistical comparisons of the risks of different energy-production technologies.

Type 2: Behavior Change and Protective Action
> Encouraging personal risk-reduction behavior.
> *Example:* Advertisements encouraging people to wear seat belts.

Type 3: Disaster Warnings and Emergency Information
> Providing direction and behavioral guidance in disasters and emergencies.
> Example: Sirens indicating the accidental release of toxic gas from a chemical plant.

Type 4: Joint Problem Solving and Conflict Resolution
> Involving the public in risk-management decision making and in resolving health, safety, and environmental controversies.
> Example: Public meetings on a possible hazardous waste site.

---

3. disaster warnings and emergency information; and

4. joint problem solving and conflict resolution.

In the real world, these four types of tasks overlap substantially, but they still can be conceptually differentiated. The task of informing and educating the public can be considered primarily a nondirective (although purposeful) activity aimed at providing the lay public with useful and enlightening information. In contrast, the tasks of encouraging behavior change and personal protective action and of providing disaster warnings and emergency information can both be considered primarily directive activities aimed at motivating people to take specific types of action. These three tasks in turn differ from the task of involving individuals and groups in joint problem solving and conflict resolution, activities in which officials and citizens exchange information and work together to solve health and environmental problems.

As is clear from the following descriptions of these four risk communication tasks, each task is also associated with a different set of characteristic problems. An extended discussion of recommendations for handling these problems can be found in the recent literature review by Covello, von Winterfeldt, and Slovic (1986).

Task Type 1: Information and Education

The following two examples are a composite of real and fictional cases and illustrate various aspects of this type of task.

Example 1. A government agency has just completed a large study comparing the risks of three methods of electricity generation: coal, nuclear power, and solar energy. Government analysts have carefully assessed and compared all available information on the health and environmental risks associated with each technology. Efforts have been made to examine a wide range of health and environmental risks, including accidents, occupational diseases, and pollution, for every facet of each technology, from the mining of raw materials to transport and production.

The study concludes that, at least for normal operations, the risks associated with nuclear power are lower than those for coal and solar energy. The findings of the study are subjected to expert peer review and published in scientific journals. Following an internal assessment of the importance of the study, the agency decides to publish its findings in a pamphlet. In the preface to the pamphlet, the agency states that its primary objective is to provide the public with up-to-date information about the relative risks of various methods of electricity generation, and not to advocate a particular form of electricity production.

Example 2. A public health official is asked to investigate a report that the groundwater near a toxic waste site may be contaminated and that, as a result, the local drinking water may also be contaminated. The community newspaper learns of the investigation and reports that the local water may be dangerous to drink. The results of the agency's investigation indicate that the local drinking water may contain up to 50 parts per billion (ppb) of a toxic chemical that has been found to produce cancer in laboratory animals. Because the level of the chemical is above health standards, the agency proposes to shut down the water supply temporarily and to provide an alternative source of water. An agency spokesperson is asked to explain the agency's position to the press.

Problems

A variety of problems complicate the task of informing and educating people about risks and risk assessment.

- Risk information is often highly technical, complex, and uncertain. Because of uncertainties deriving from a lack of scientific data and from deficiencies in available methods and models, it is not uncommon to find substantial variations in risk estimates. For example, a committee of the National Academy of Sciences (1978) estimated that the expected number of bladder cancers resulting from the consumption of saccharin over the next 70 years ranges from between 0.22 and 1,144,000 cases, depending on the assumptions made.

- Experts often disagree on the assumptions underlying a risk assessment and, as a result, often provide widely different risk estimates. One result of these disagreements is public confusion about the validity of risk estimates.

- Regulatory agencies, like experts, sometimes lack public trust and credibility. Trust and credibility can be undermined by many factors, including public perceptions that an agency lacks technical competence, that agency decisions are overly influenced by special-interest groups, or that an agency is inappropriately biased in favor of a particular technology or political strategy.

- Experts and laypeople often define risk differently. Experts typically define risk strictly in terms of expected annual mortalities. Laypeople almost always include other factors in their definition of risk, such as catastrophic potential, equity (that is, whether those receiving benefits from a particular technology or action bear their share of the risks), effects on future generations, controllability, and involuntariness. As a result of these differing definitions, laypeople tend to assign relatively little weight to risk assessments conducted by technical experts and government agencies.

- Government officials often use technical, legalistic, or bureaucratic language in describing or discussing risk. Besides being difficult to comprehend, such language gives the impression that officials are being unresponsive or evasive. For example, an official's statement that "groundwater contamination of 5 parts per billion is within the limits of acceptable safety standards set by the agency" may be technically correct but may also leave individuals suspicious and confused about the meaning of this statement and its relevance to a particular situation. Government officials may argue that technical language is unavoidable, given the constraints placed on them by the nature of the data, by agency regulations, and by the law.

- Individuals are frequently unwilling to believe officials who claim that their decisions and actions are so constrained. Individuals who are directly affected by a government decision are especially reluctant to accept such claims and often demand that a risk agent be banned or a hazardous activity curtailed.

- People are often not as interested in risk problems as are officials in government agencies. Given competing interests and priorities, issues that are high on the agendas of government agencies may be low on the agendas of average citizens. It may thus be difficult to get people to pay attention to risk information. Those individuals who do pay attention may be highly selective and may focus on unusual and dramatic aspects of the problem instead of on representative data and statistics.

- Risk information can be frightening. Statements by a government official meant to assure the public that its water is safe to drink, its air safe to breathe, or its food safe to eat may have exactly the opposite effect. Instead of alleviating concern, such statements may increase fear, anxiety, and avoidance of an activity previously assumed to be safe. The very fact that an official investigation is under way may be sufficient to create an atmosphere of fear and suspicion.

- People holding strong beliefs are exceedingly resistant to changing such beliefs, even when confronted with substantial and opposing scientific evidence. Motorcyclists, for example, often deny that they engage in a high-risk activity even when presented with statistics on the high incidence of motorcycle accidents. Such persons frequently question the accuracy of the statistics or the relevance of the statistics to their own situation. For example, some motorcyclists may refer to their superior abilities and experience in handling motorcycles or their accident-free records. The other side of the issue of belief is that individuals with weakly held beliefs can often be manipulated by subtle differences in the presentation of risk information.

- Most people have difficulty interpreting probabilistic information. Extremely small probabilities, such as a chance of one in a million or smaller, are especially difficult to comprehend.

Relevant Research

Of the various academic disciplines concerned with problems related to information and education, researchers in the fields of cognitive and social psychology have been among the most active.[1] Cognitive and social psychologists have explored questions such as these: How do people define and perceive risks, and what determines a risk's acceptability? Does newspaper coverage bias the perception of risks? What are the determinants of attitudes and attitude change? What factors influence the success or failure of educational efforts? How does the presentation of risk information influence perceptions and preferences?

Sociologists, economists, political scientists, anthropologists, health educators, and communications researchers have also been active in the study of problems related to information and education. Psychologists have usually focused on the mental processing and evaluation of risk information. Sociologists, economists, political scientists, anthropologists, and health educators have focused on the influence of social, economic, institutional, organizational, or cultural factors, as well as the influence of the media on risk perceptions, preferences, and behavioral responses to risk-related information.[2]

Conclusions

Several general conclusions can be drawn from the literature on informing and educating people about risk. To perform this task effectively, communicators should attempt to do the following:
- Use simple, graphic, and concrete material, avoiding technical or specialized language wherever possible.
- Compare risks within a carefully defined context that is relevant to the target audience.
- Avoid comparisons of risks that may appear to the audience to be noncomparable because of different qualitative characteristics—for example, the risk of smoking compared to that of living near a nuclear power plant.
- Understand and recognize qualitative concerns, such as concerns about catastrophic potential, dread, equity, and controllability.
- Identify and explain the strengths and limitations of different risk

measures, and present (whenever possible) alternative measures and indexes of risk—for example, measures of expected fatalities or incidences of disease for the entire population and for the most- and least-exposed individuals.

- Identify, acknowledge, and explain uncertainties in risk estimates.
- Provide opportunities for people to learn how to interpret risk information.
- Relate on a personal level—that is, when people ask personal questions such as "Can I drink the water?" respond in a personal way without minimizing risks and uncertainties.
- Recognize the power of subtle changes in the way information is presented and use such knowledge responsibly.
- Understand and recognize that health and environmental debates often involve much broader considerations, including political values and ideologies.

Task Type 2: Behavior Change and Protective Action

The following two examples are a composite of real and fictional cases and illustrate various aspects of this type of task.

Example 1. A government agency has finished reviewing research that indicates a high-cholesterol diet increases arteriosclerosis and leads to heart attacks and strokes. On the basis of the evidence, the agency decides to launch a campaign encouraging people to adopt a low-cholesterol diet. It contracts with a large advertising agency to develop a series of pamphlets aimed at several select population groups, such as the young and those who already have cardiovascular problems.

Example 2. A state highway safety agency is concerned about increasing numbers of highway deaths. It plans a media advertising campaign aimed at discouraging drunk driving during an upcoming holiday period. The agency enlists the support of local television stations in broadcasting a series of public-service announcements. The announcements include messages that stress (1) the greater risks of being arrested for drunk driving during the holiday period because of increases in police surveillance and highway checkpoints; (2) the responsibility of friends and relatives in preventing individuals from driving while intoxicated; and (3) the consequences of drunk driving, as shown through graphic photographs of highway automobile accidents.

Problems

In addition to problems already noted in relation to the first communication task, a variety of problems complicate the task of encouraging behavior change and protective action.

- The losses incurred by individuals who change their behavior, such as the loss of the pleasure of smoking or the taste of a favorite food, are tangible and immediate; in contrast, the gains are abstract, intangible, and remote in time.
- People frequently display an "optimism bias"—for example, a belief that fate or luck is on their side or that "it can't happen to me," so as to avoid a behavior change. This is especially true of individuals engaged in activities that require skill and involve individual control, such as driving or skiing.
- People also rationalize their resistance to behavior change. For example, smokers who need the psychological relief of smoking a cigarette often cite the pressures of modern life as a justification and minimize the risks.
- People often resist government efforts aimed at changing behavior for political or ideological reasons. For many, such efforts represent unacceptable intrusions by government in their personal lives.
- The target audience of a behavior-change campaign is often unmotivated and uninvolved; consequently, it may ignore the campaign's message. This has been shown in campaigns aimed at encouraging people to use seat belts and to improve their diet.
- Individuals seldom respond appropriately to high-threat or fear-evoking communications, such as photographs or films graphically depicting the physical symptoms of disease or the results of a disfiguring or fatal accident. Such communications may induce excessive fear and anxiety, which may in turn reduce attention, prompt defensive responses, and evoke hostility toward the source of the communication.

Relevant Research

Of the various academic disciplines concerned with problems of behavior change and protective action, researchers in the fields of consumer behavior, marketing, advertising, social psychology, sociology, health promotion, and disease prevention have been among the most active.[3] Researchers in consumer behavior, marketing, and advertising have been concerned primarily with factors that underlie consumer choice. Social psychologists, sociologists, and health promotion specialists have been interested primarily in attitude change and persuasion, as well as in the social and institutional processes that precede behavior change.

Conclusions

Several general conclusions can be drawn from the literature on the task of encouraging behavior change and protective action. To perform the task effectively, communicators should attempt to do the following:

- Identify a specific target audience and tailor the communication to that audience.
- Generate involvement by creating vivid, concrete images that the target audience can relate to on a personal level.
- Use innovative ways to attract the attention of the target audience.
- Avoid high-threat or fear-evoking campaigns; present a moderate position and carefully develop the argument.
- Use multiple channels and media—for example, newspapers, television, magazines, films, school presentations, and pamphlets in doctors' offices and hospital waiting rooms.
- Present recommendations in the context of a balanced argument that accurately describes the strengths and weaknesses of both sides, especially if the target audience is likely to be exposed to strong counterarguments and recommendations.
- Build on expertise, trust, and credibility: people are more willing to accept a communication if the communicator is believed to be knowledgeable, respected, unbiased, and truthful.

Task Type 3: Disaster Warnings and Emergency Information

The following two examples are a composite of real and fictional cases and illustrate various aspects of this type of task.

Example 1. A community is struck by a small earthquake, and experts believe that a larger earthquake is likely to occur within six months. The exact date of the expected earthquake is, however, highly uncertain. Local police and fire departments are informed, and the media are provided information about emergency preparedness. When the earthquake finally occurs, it is much larger than anticipated and results in a massive breakdown in communications.

Example 2. A government agency is called in to deal with an accident that has occurred at a large industrial chemical facility. Emergency operations are under way, and a press conference has been called to inform the public about the state of the facility, reasons for the accident, actions being taken, extent of the damage, risks of further complications, and the need for possible evacuation. The situation is tense and compounded by rumors and conflicting information from several sources.

Problems

In addition to problems already noted in relation to the preceding communication tasks, a variety of problems complicate the task of providing disaster warnings and emergency information.

- In most disasters and emergencies, the primary objectives of government officials are to minimize loss of life and to minimize property damage. These macro-objectives often come into conflict with the micro-objectives of local residents (and sometimes local disaster or emergency workers), who frequently assign highest priority to the protection of their own family members, friends, personal possessions, and property.
- Time pressures often compound an already difficult situation.
- Coordination among agencies and organizations frequently breaks down during disasters. Confusion about responsibility and authority often results in multiple and competing sources of information.
- Communication channels, too, frequently break down during disasters and may result in confusion and the spread of rumors.
- Warning systems frequently produce false alarms, which confuse people, generate mistrust in the warning system, and may desensitize people to future warnings.
- Individuals often deny the possibility of a disaster or do not believe that it may affect them personally. Thus, it is often difficult to capture public interest and attention before a disaster occurs. (These observations appear to apply more to natural disasters than to technological disasters.)
- Once a disaster occurs, people are sometimes reluctant to evacuate, especially in natural disasters; concerns about the loss of personal belongings and of opportunities to save homes and property often outweigh the motivation to evacuate.
- People usually require confirmation of the original emergency communication through several channels (for example, through

telephone calls to the local police or to friends) before taking action. However, these channels often break down during a disaster or emergency. Without the ability to confirm the original message, people may become confused and not act appropriately.

Relevant Research

Of the various academic disciplines concerned with disaster warnings and emergency information, sociological and social psychological researchers have been among the most active. The literature includes general reviews,[4] case studies of risk communication prior to and during disasters and emergencies,[5] and studies of specific aspects of the disaster process, such as warning systems,[6] media coverage,[7] and evacuation behavior.[8]

Conclusions

Several general conclusions can be drawn from the literature on disaster warnings and emergency information. To perform this task effectively, communicators should attempt to do the following:

- Provide concrete information about specific actions individuals can take.
- Transmit official communications through a single, reliable, respected, and highly credible spokesperson.
- Be sensitive to the possibility of overloading people with too much information.
- Use multiple channels (such as radio, television, pamphlets, sound trucks, and door-to-door canvassing) for communicating.
- Allow for individuals' need to confirm disaster and emergency information.
- Establish hot lines for rumor control.
- Design communications that are sensitive to the fears and concerns of local residents and that provide information specifically addressing these concerns.
- Design warning systems that can remain credible even if the threat does not materialize.
- Involve local citizens in the design of programs aimed at providing disaster warnings and emergency information.

Task Type 4: Joint Problem Solving and Conflict Resolution

The following two examples are a composite of real and fictional cases and illustrate various aspects of this type of task.

Example 1. An agency official wishes to secure greater public involvement in the risk management decisions facing the agency. As preparation, the official reviews upcoming decisions facing the agency and identifies a particularly difficult one concerning a chemical plant in a small city that is highly dependent on the plant for jobs. According to agency experts, the chemical plant is not in compliance with agency regulations on toxic emissions and will not be able to meet prescribed levels even after installing advanced technological controls. The agency official sees two main policy options: tolerate the emissions or order the plant to close down. Given this dilemma, the official appeals to the citizens of the city to express their views, through workshops and public meetings, on the agency's policy options as well as on alternative approaches. The official hopes that these meetings will result in a broad and direct exchange of information between the agency and the community.

Example 2. A toxic waste site is declared hazardous to human health, and the department of public health sends in experts and public involvement specialists to work with local residents in finding a solution. In the first meeting, residents criticize the agency for foot dragging and demand that the site be immediately cleaned up, regardless of costs. The situation becomes especially tense when a young woman who lives near the site claims that drinking water contaminated by the site caused her recent miscarriage.

Problems

In addition to the problems already noted in relation to the three other communication tasks, a variety of problems complicate the task of involving the public in joint problem solving and conflict resolution.

- Actions by a government agency aimed at involving the public in the regulatory decision-making process may be viewed as an attempt by the agency to abdicate its legal duties and responsibilities. This problem is compounded by the fact that individuals and groups are often asked to participate in the decision-making process only after many of the most important decisions have already been made, which prompts even greater skepticism on the part of those inclined to view the process as a form of rubber-stamping.

- It is difficult to hold public meetings in a highly charged, emotional atmosphere. A common characteristic of joint problem-solving exercises is strong involvement by groups with a stake in the issue, each group bringing its own values and concerns to the arena. Frequently, the initial atmosphere is one of distrust and confrontation rather than openness and cooperation.
- Agency officials often do not understand the nature of a particular conflict or the sources of a particular disagreement. Disagreements can range from factual disputes about levels of risk to fundamental disagreements over values and ethical principles.
- Many communication strategies are inappropriate for specific types of conflict. For example, when conflicts are about facts and statistics, information and education strategies are relevant. However, when conflicts are about the equity (fairness) of risk/benefit distributions or about basic values, education and information strategies are of little value. Such cases require careful diagnosis of the concerns of all interested parties and the design of options (such as safeguards or compensation schemes) that specifically address these concerns.
- Individuals and groups involved in the decision-making process are often unwilling to compromise or accept trade-offs. For example, local residents may exhibit a "not-in-my-backyard" attitude when exposed to a new risk and frequently demand complete elimination of the risk regardless of costs, resources, or other constraints.
- The media may aggravate communication problems by highlighting personal fears and anxieties, by focusing only on the dramatic or sensational aspects of an episode or event, and by emphasizing conflict rather than agreement.

Relevant Research

Of the various academic disciplines concerned with joint problem solving and conflict resolution, researchers in the fields of decision science, political science, and sociology have been among the most active. Within these disciplines, specialists in public involvement and social conflict have been especially productive. Public involvement studies have examined numerous examples of interactions between the public and government agencies.[9] Researchers have also drawn on the literature of game and decision theory[10] and on that of bargaining, negotiation, and mediation[11] to develop tools for diagnosing the nature of conflicts among groups and mechanisms for resolving conflicts. Three additional research traditions have also made substantial contributions: sociological research on the causes and dynamics of technological controversies,[12] research on environmental mediation and arbitration,[13] and research on consent and decision making.[14]

Conclusions

Several general conclusions can be drawn from the literature on involving the public in joint problem solving and conflict resolution. To perform this task effectively, communicators should attempt to do the following:

- Involve the public early in decision making—that is, before assumptions have been made, alternatives narrowed, and key decisions made, and before decision makers have become committed to a particular course of action.
- Make the objectives for involving the public clear from the beginning.
- Leave room for option invention by those directly involved with or affected by the decision.
- Understand and respect individual interests, emotions, values, priorities, preferences, and concerns.
- In public meetings, identify with the audience and avoid violations of community norms regarding dress, language, and demeanor.
- Establish elaborate procedural safeguards to ensure that all voices with an interest or stake in the decision can be heard.
- Carefully analyze the nature of conflicts and distinguish between different types of conflict—for example, distinguish factual disagreements from deeply rooted ideological conflicts.
- Adopt different communication strategies for different types of conflict and disagreement.

Cross-Cutting Conclusions

Several general conclusions can be drawn from the literature that cut across all four types of communication tasks. These are briefly discussed below. They are followed by four basic messages, directed at risk communicators, which emerge from the literature.

- The roots of most risk communication problems lie in the complexities of the risk problem itself. What sometimes appears to be a simple and direct issue often turns out to be one of enormous scientific, economic, social, and political complexity. Limitations in the science of risk assessment, in public perceptions and understanding, in media coverage, in risk management institutions, and in economic and other resources pose serious obstacles to risk communication. Without awareness and recognition of these obstacles, effective communication is unlikely.

- Interactive and participatory approaches to risk communication appear to offer the greatest promise of better, less controversial, or less divisive decisions. Even the most directive types of risk communication tasks, such as encouraging personal behavior change and providing disaster warnings, can benefit substantially from public involvement, direct interaction, and exchanges of information. Such interactions are an important source of knowledge of public needs and concerns, without which communication efforts are likely to fail or be ineffective.

- There is no such entity as "the public." Instead, there are many publics, each with its own interests, needs, concerns, priorities, and preferences.

- Communication problems can often be viewed beneficially as decision-making problems. For example, the choice of one communication strategy over another can often be illuminated through a formal analysis of the multiple competing factors that might be considered in making the decision, including the community's "right to know," the duty to protect public health, the costs of unnecessarily alarming people, and the possible repercussions of premature or delayed action.

- Government officials and individual citizens often hold different views of risk problems. Most federal regulatory agencies view risk problems from a societal or macro-perspective. As a result, most analyses by government agencies provide only aggregate or population statistics for the community or nation as a whole. Aggregate or population statistics are, however, usually of little interest to individual citizens, who are most likely to view risks from a micro-perspective and to be more concerned about risks to themselves or to their loved ones than about risks to society or the community as a whole. Given this divergence of viewpoints, government officials are often at a disadvantage, as they typically do not have immediate access to information that addresses the highly personalized questions asked by citizens.

- A large amount of research has been conducted that bears on problems of risk communication, but the literature specifically focused on risk communication is relatively small. Substantial progress has been made on some topics, such as psychological research on public perceptions of risk, but large gaps exist in our understanding of virtually every issue relevant to risk communication. Institutional arrangements and financial resources for research on risk communication issues are inadequate.

Four main messages specifically directed at risk communicators emerge from the literature:

1. Know your risk communication problems.
2. Know your risk communication objectives.
3. Use simple and nontechnical language.
4. Listen to your audience and know its concerns.

The first two messages point to the importance of understanding the unique characteristics of the risk communication tasks and underscore the importance of being clear about the nature of the problem and about the intent of the communication. The last two messages underscore the importance of adopting a communication approach that is appropriate to the specific problem and the specific audience.

Many of the recommendations in this paper may seem obvious, but they are nonetheless continually and consistently violated. These violations make effective communication about health and environmental risks unnecessarily difficult.

NOTES

The views and conclusions expressed in this appendix are solely those of the authors and do not necessarily reflect the views and conclusions of the National Science Foundation.

1. See, for example, Combs and Slovic, 1979; Slovic et al., 1978, 1979, 1980, 1981, 1982; Green, 1980; Johnson and Tversky, 1983; McNeil et al., 1982; Renn, 1981; Fischhoff et al., 1978, 1979, 1984; Lichtenstein et al., 1978; Otway, 1980; Otway and von Winterfeldt, 1982; Otway et al., 1978; Tversky and Kahneman, 1981; von Winterfeldt et al., 1981; Vlek and Stallen, 1981; Squyres, 1980; Gardner et al., 1982; Lowrance, 1976; Kasperson and Kasperson, 1983; Covello, 1983, 1984.

2. See, for example, Conrad, 1980; Mazur, 1973, 1981; Nelkin, 1984; Nelkin and Brown, 1984; Perrow, 1984; Wildavsky and Douglas, 1982; Gross and Rayner, 1983;

Twentieth-Century Fund, 1984; Mitchell, 1980; Short, 1984; Douglas, 1966; Rothman, 1982; Sharlin, 1985; Levine, 1982; Shelanski et al., 1982; Winsten, 1985; Sandman, 1973, 1975, 1982; Sandman and Pden, 1979; Johnson and Covello, 1986; Morris et al., 1980; Lipset and Schneider, 1983; Barber 1983; Short, 1984; Burger, 1984; Media Institute, 1985.

3. See, for example, McGuire 1985; Eagly and Chaiken, 1985; Earle and Cvetkovich, 1983; Earle, 1984; Vertinsky and Vertinsky, 1982; Weinstein, 1984; Maccoby et al., Maccoby and Solomon, 1977, 1981; Fishbein and Ajzen, 1975; Kiesler et al., 1968, Gusfield, 1982; Robinson, 1976; Robinson et al., 1974; Sutton, 1982; Alcalay, 1983; Adler and Pittle, 1984; Evans and Clarke, 1983; Rice and Page, 1981.

4. See, for example, Mileti et al., 1975; Quarantelli and Dynes, 1977; Kreps, 1984; Saarinen, 1982.

5. See, for example, Cutter and Barnes, 1982; Friedman, 1981; Greene et al., 1980; Kunreuther et al., 1978; Lindell et al., 1983; Lagadec, 1982; Shelanski, 1982; Bowonder, 1985.

6. See, for example, Mileti, 1975; Turner et al., 1981; Nilson and Nilson, 1981; Hodler, 1982; Pate-Cornell, 1986.

7. See, for example, Mazur, 1981; Mazur et al., 1982; Rogers and Sood, 1986; Sandman, 1979; Peltu, 1985.

8. See, for example, Perry et al., 1980; Lindell et al., 1985; Quarantelli, 1980.

9. See, for example, Creighton, 1980; Delli Priscoli et al., 1983; Popper, 1985; Susskind, 1978; Susskind et al., 1978.

10. See, for example, Luce and Raiffa, 1957; Keeney and Raiffa, 1976; von Winterfeldt and Edwards, 1985.

11. See, for example, Raiffa, 1982.

12. See, for example, Tribe et al., 1976; Coser, 1956; Mazur, 1980, 1981; Nelkin, 1978; Ferrow, 1984.

13. See, for example, Busterud, 1980; Bingham, 1984; Cormick, 1980; Wellborn, 1979; O'Hare, 1977, 1984; Susskind and Wheeler, 1983; Bacow et al., 1983; Bacow and Wheeler, 1983; Mernitz, 1980.

14. See, for example, Gibson, 1985; MacLean, 1986.

BIBLIOGRAPHY

Adler, R., and Pittle, R. D. "Cajolery or Command: Are Education Campaigns an Adequate Substitute for Regulation?" *Yale Journal on Regulation* 1 (1984):159-193.

Alcalay, R. "The Impact of Mass Communication in the Health Field." *Social Science and Medicine* 17 (1983):87-94.

Barber, B. *The Logic and Limits of Trust*. New Brunswick, N.J.: Rutgers University Press, 1983.

Bingham, G. *Resolving Environmental Disputes: A Decade of Experience*. Washington, D.C.: The Conservation Foundation, 1984.

Bowonder, B. "Low-Probability Event: A Case Study in Risk Assessment." Paper presented at the workshop on "Risk Analysis in Developing Countries." Hyderabad, India, October 1985.

Burger, E. *Health Risks: The Challenges of Informing the Public.* Washington, D.C.: The Media Institute, 1984.

Busterud, J. "Mediation: The State of the Art." *Environmental Professional* 2 (1980):34-39.

Combs, B. and Slovic P. "Newspaper Coverage of Causes of Death." *Journalism Quarterly* 56 (1979):837-843.

Covello, V. T. "The Perception of Technological Risks: A Literature Review." *Technological Forecasting and Social Change* 23 (1983):285-297.

Covello, V. T. "Uses of Social and Behavioral Research on Risk." *Environment International* (June 1984).

Covello, V. T., von Winterfeldt, D., and Slovic, P. *Risk Communication: Background Report for the National Conference on Risk Communication.* Washington, D.C.: The Conservation Foundation, 1986.

Conrad, J., ed. *Society, Technology, and Risk Assessment.* New York: Academic Press, 1980.

Cormick, G. W. "The Theory and Practice of Environmental Mediation." *Environmental Professional* 2 (1980):24- 33.

Coser, L. A. *The Functions of Social Conflict.* New York: Free Press, 1956.

Creighton, J. L. *Public Involvement Manual: Involving the Public in Water and Power Resource Discussions.* Washington, D.C.: U.S. Government Printing Office, 1980.

Cutter, S., and Barnes, K. "Evacuation Behavior and Three Mile Island." *Disasters* 6 (1982):116-124.

Delli Priscoli, J. Creighton, J., and Dunning, C. M., ed. *Public Involvement Techniques: A Reader of Ten Years Experience of Institute for Water Resources.* U.S. Army Corps of Engineers, Institute for Water Resources, Washington, D.C.: 1983. IWR Research Report 82-R1.

Douglas, M. *Purity and Danger.* London: Routledge and Kegan Paul, 1966.

Douglas, M., and Wildavsky, A. *Risk and Culture.* Berkeley, Calif.: University of California Press, 1982.

Eagly, A. H., and Chaiken, S. "Psychological Theories of Persuasion." In Berkowitz, L., ed. *Advances in Experimental Social Psychology.* 1985.

Earle, T. C. "Risk Communication: A Marketing Approach." Unpublished paper presented at the National Science Foundation/Environmental Protection Agency Workshop on Risk Perception and Risk Communication, Long Beach, Calif. (December 1984).

Earle, T. C., and Cvetkovich, G. "Risk Judgment and the Communication of Hazard Information: Toward a New Look in the Study of Risk Perception." BH ARC (400/83/017). Seattle: Battelle Human Affairs Research Centers, 1983.

Evans, S. H., and Clarke, P. "When Cancer Patients Fail to Get Well: Flaws in Health Communication." In Bostrom, R. N., ed. *Communication Yearbook 7.* Beverly Hills, Calif.: Sage, 1983.

Fischhoff, B., et al. "How Safe is Safe Enough? A Psychometric Study of Attitudes Towards Technological Risks and Benefits." *Policy Sciences* 8 (1978):127-52.

Fischhoff, B., Slovic, P., and Lichtenstein, S. "Weighing the Risks." *Environment* 21 (1979):17-10, 32-38.

Fischhoff, B., Watson, S., and Hope, C. "Defining Risk." *Policy Sciences* 17 (1984):123-139.

Fishbein, M., and Ajzen, I. *Belief, Attitude, Intention and Behavior: An Introduction to Theory and Research.* Reading, Mass.: Addison-Wesley, 1975.

Friedman, S. M. "Blueprint for Breakdown: Three Mile Island and the Mass Media Before the Accident." *Journal of Communications* 31 (1981):85-96.

Gibson, M., ed. *To Breathe Freely: Risk, Consent, and Air.* Totowa, N.J.: Rowman and Allanheld, 1985.

Green, C. H. "Risk: Attitudes and Beliefs." In Canter, D. V., ed. *Behavior in Fires.* Chichester, England: John Wiley, 1980.

Greene, M., Perry, R. W., and Lindell, M. K. "The March 1980 Eruptions of Mount St. Helens: Citizens Perceptions of Volcano Hazard." *Disasters* (1980):49-66.

Gross, J. L., and Rayner, S. *Measuring Culture: A Paradigm for the Analysis of Social Organization.* New York: Columbia University Press, 1983.

Hoder, T. W. "Residents' Preparedness and Response to the Kalamazoo Tornado." *Disasters* 2 (1982):44-49.

Johnson, B., and Covello, V., eds. *The Social Construction of Risk.* Boston: Reidel, 1986.

Johnson, E. J., and Tversky, A. "Affect, Generalization, and the Perception of Risk." *Journal of Personality and Social Psychology* 45 (1983):20-31.

Kasperson, R., and Kasperson, J. "Determining the Acceptability of Risk: Ethical and Policy Issues." In Rogers, J., and Bates, D., eds. *Risk: A Symposium.* Ottawa: The Royal Society of Canada.

Keeney, R. L., and Raiffa, H. *Decisions with Multiple Objectives: Preferences and Value Tradeoffs.* New York: John Wiley, 1976.

Kiesler, C. A., Collins, B. E., and Miller, N. *Attitude Change.* New York: John Wiley, 1968.

Kunreuther, H., et al. *Disaster Insurance Protection: Public Policy Lessons.* New York: John Wiley, 1978.

Lagadec, P. *Major Technological Disaster.* Oxford, England: Pergamon Press: 1982.

Levine, A. G. *Love Canal: Science, Politics, and People.* Lexington, Mass.: D.C. Heath, 1982.

Lichtenstein, S., et al. "Judged Frequently of Lethal Events." *Journal of Experimental Psychology: Human Learning and Memory* 4 (1978):551-578.

Lindell, M., et al. *Planning Concepts and Decision Criteria for Sheltering and Evacuation in a Nuclear Power Plant Emergency.* Technical Report No AIF/NESP-031. Seattle: Battelle Human Affairs Research Centers, 1985.

Lipset, S., and Schneider, W. *The Confidence Gap: Business Labor and Government in the Public Mind.* New York: Free Press, 1983.

Lowrance, W. *Of Acceptable Risk: Science and the Determination of Safety.* Los Altos, Calif.: Kaufman, 1976.

Luce, D. and Raiffa, H. *Games and Decisions.* New York: John Wiley, 1957.

Maccoby, N., Farquhar, J., Wood, P., and Alexander, J. "Reducing the Risk of Cardiovascular Disease: Effects of a Community- Based Campaign on Knowledge and Behavior." *Journal of Community Health* (1977).

Maccoby, N., and Solomon, D. S. "Heart Disease Prevention: Community Studies." In Rice, R. E., and Paisley, W. J. eds. *Public Communication Campaigns*. Beverly Hills, Calif.: Russell Sage, 1981.

MacLean, D., ed. *Values at Risk*. Totowa, N.J.: Rowman and Allanheld, 1986.

Mazur, A., "Disputes Between Experts." *Minerva* 11 (1973):243-262.

Mazur, A. *The Dynamics of Technical Controversy*. Washington, D.C.: Communications Press, 1981.

Mazur, A. "Media Coverage and Public Opinion on Scientific Controversies." *Journal of Communications Research* 31 (1980):106-115.

Media Institute. *Chemical Risks: Fears, Facts, and the Media*. Washington, D.C.: Media Institute, 1985.

Mileti, D. *Natural Hazard Warning Systems in the U.S.: A Research Assessment*. Technical Report, Institute for Behavioral Science. Boulder, Col.: University of Colorado, 1975.

Mileti, D., Drabek, T., and Haas, E. *Human Behavior in Extreme Environments*. Boulder, Col.: University of Colorado, 1975.

McGuire, W. J. "Attitudes and Attitude Change.: In Lindzey and Aronson, eds. *Handbook of Social Psychology*. 1985.

McNeil, B. J., Pauker, S. G., Sox, H. C., Jr., and Tversky, A. "On the Elicitation of Preference for Alternative Therapies." *New England Journal of Medicine* 306 (1982):1259-1262.

Mitchell, R. C. *Public Opinion on Environmental Issues: Results of a National Public Opinion Survey*. Washington, D.C.: Council on Environmental Quality, 1980.

Morris, L., Mazis, M., and Barofsky, I., eds. *Product Labeling and Health Risks*. Banbury Report 6. Cold Spring Harbor, N.Y.: Cold Spring Harbor Laboratory, 1980.

National Academy of Sciences/National Research Council. *Saccharin: Technical Assessment of Risks and Benefits. Committee for a study on saccharin and food safety policy*. Washington, D.C.: National Academy of Sciences, 1978. (Second Edition.) Sage: Beverly Hills, 1984.

Nelkin, D., ed. *Controversy: Politics of Technical Decisions*. Beverly Hills, Calif.: Russell Sage, 1978.

Nelkin, D., and Brown M. *Workers at Risk: Voices from the Workplace*. Chicago: University of Chicago Press, 1984.

Nilson, L. B., and Nilson, D. C. "Resolving the 'sooner vs. later' controversy surrounding the public announcement of earthquake predictions." *Disasters* 5 (1981):391-397.

O'Hare, M. "Not on my Block You Don't: Facility Siting and the Strategic Importance of Compensation." *Public Policy* 197, 25 (1977):407-458.

O'Hare, M. "Bargaining and Negotiation for a Conflict Resolution." In Kunreuther, H., and Kleindorfer, P., eds. *Production, Transportation, and Storage of Hazardous Materials*. New York: Springer, 1976.

Otway, H., Maurer, D., and Thomas, K. "Nuclear Power: The Question of Public Acceptance." *Future* 10 (1978):109-118.

Otway, H. J. "Risk Perception: A Psychological Perspective." In Dierkes, M., Edwards, S., and Coppock, R. eds. *Technical Risk: Its Perspective and Handling in Europe*. Boston: Oelgeschlager, Gunn and Hain, 1980.

Otway, H. J., and von Winterfeldt, D. "Beyond Acceptable Risk: On the Social Acceptability of Technologies." *Policy Sciences* 8 (1982):127-152.

Pate-Cornell, M. E. "Warning Systems in Risk Management." *Risk Analysis* 6, 2 (1986).

Peltu, M. E. "Risk Communication: The Role of the Media." In Otway, H., ed *Risk and Regulation*. London: Butterworths, 1985.

Perrow, C. *Normal Accidents*. New York: Basic Books, 1984.

Perry, R. W., Greene, M. R., and Lindell, M. K. "Enhancing Evacuation Warning Compliance: Suggestions for Emergency Planning." *Disasters* 4 (1980: 433-449.

Popper, F. "The Environmentalists and the LULU (Local Unwanted Land Use). *Environment* (March 1985).

Quarantelli, E., and Dynes, R. "Response to Social Crisis and Disaster." *Annual Review of Sociology* 3 (1977):23- 49.

Quarantelli, E. L. *Evacuation Behavior and Problems: Findings and Implications from the Research Literature*. Department of Sociology, Disaster Research Centers. Columbus, Ohio: Ohio State University, 1980.

Raiffa, H. *The Art and Science of Negotiation*. Cambridge, Mass.: Harvard University Press, 1982.

Renn, O. Man, Technology, and Risk: A Study on Intuitive Risk Assessment and Attitudes Towards Nuclear Power. Report Jul- Spez 115, Julich. Nuclear Research Center, 1981.

Rice, E. E. and Paisley, W. J., eds. *Public Communication Campaigns*. Beverly Hills, Calif.: Russell Sage, 1981.

Robertson, L. "The Great Seat Belt Campaign Flop." *Journal of Communication* 26 (1976):41-45.

Robertson, L., et al. "A Controlled Study of the Effect of Television Messages on Safety Belt Use." *American Journal of Public Health* 64(1974):1071-1081.

Rogers, E. M., and Sood, R. "Mass Media Operations in a Quick Onset Natural Disaster: Hurricane David in Dominica." Working Paper, Annenberg School of Communications. Los Angeles: University of Southern California, 1981.

Rothman, S. Risk and Nuclear Power: Scientists, Journalists, and the Public. *Public Opinion* (1982):47-52.

Ruckelshaus, W. "Risk in a Free Society." *Risk Analysis* 4, 3 (1984):157-163.

Saarinen, T., ed. *Perspectives on Increasing Hazard Awareness*. Boulder, Col.: Institute of Behavioral Science, 1982.

Sandman, P. M., and Paden, M. "At Three Mile Island." *Columbia Journalism Review* 18, 2 (1979):43-58.

Sandman, P. "Environmental Advertising and Social Responsibility." In Rubin, D.. and Sachs, D., eds. *Mass Media and the Environment*. New York: Praeger, 1973.

Sharlin, H. I. *EDB: A Case Study in the Communication of Health Risk*. Unpublished manuscript commissioned by the Office of Policy Agency, U.S. Environmental Protection Agency, Washington, D.C., January 1985.

Shelanski, V., Sills, D., and Wolf, C. *The Accident at Three Mile Island*. Boulder, Col.: Westview Press, 1982.

Short, J. "The Social Fabric of Risk." *American Sociological Review* (December 1984).

Slovic, P., Lichtenstein, S., and Fischoff, B. "Images of Disaster: Perceptions and

Acceptance of Risks from Nuclear Power." In Goodman, G. and Rowe, W., eds. ✓
Energy Risk Management. London: Academic Press, 1979.

Slovic, P., Fischhoff, B., and Lichtenstein, S. "Facts and Fears: Understanding Perceived Risk." In Schwing, R. and Albers, W. A., eds. Social Risk Assessment: How Safe Is Safe Enough? New York: Plenum, 1980. Revision in Kahneman, D., Slovic, P., and Tversky, A., eds. Judgment under Uncertainty: Heuristics and Biases. New York: Cambridge University Press, 1982.

Slovic, P., Fischhoff, B., and Lichtenstein, S. "Informing People about Risk." In Morris, ⌐ L., Mazis, M., and Barofsky, I., eds. Product Labeling and Health Risks. Banbury Report 6. Cold Spring Harbor, N.Y.:1980. The Banbury Center, 1980.

Slovic, P., Fischhoff, B., and Lichtenstein, S. "Perceived Risk: Psychological Factors, and Social Implications." In Warner, F. and Slater D. H., eds. The Assessment and Perception of Risk. London: The Royal Society, 1981.

Squyres, W. D. Patient Education: New York: Springer, 1980.

Susskind, L. E. The Importance of Citizen Participation and Consensus-Building in the Land Use Planning Process. Cambridge, Mass.: Massachusetts Institute of Technology, Laboratory of Architecture and Planning, 1978.

Susskind, L., Richardson, J. R., and Hildebrand, K. Resolving Environmental Disputes: Approaches to Intervention, Negotiation, and Conflict Resolution. Environmental Impact Assessment Project, Cambridge, Mass.: Massachusetts Institute of Technology, 1978.

Sutton, S. R. "Fear Arousing Communications: A Critical Examination of Theory and Research." In Eiser, J. R. ed. Social Psychology and Behavioral Medicine. New York: John Wiley, 1982.

Tribe, L. H., Corrine, S., Shelling T., and Voss, eds. When Values Conflict: Essays on Environmental Analysis, Discourses and Decision. Cambridge, Mass.: Ballinger, 1976.

Turner, R. H., Nigg, J. M., Paz, D. H., and Young, B. S. Community Response to Earthquake Threat in Southern California Institute for Social Science Research. Los Angeles, Calif.: University of California, 1981.

Tversky, A., and Kahneman, D. "The framing of decisions and the Psychology of Choice." Science 211 (1981):235-271.

Twentieth Century Fund. Science in the Streets. New York: Priority Press, 1984.

U.S. Environmental Protection Agency, Risk Assessment and Risk Management: Framework for Decision Making. Washington, D.C.: U.S. Environmental Protection Agency, 1984.

Vertinsky, I., and Vertinsky, P. "Communicating Environmental Health Assessment and Other Risk Information: Analysis of Strategies." In Kunreuther, H., ed. Risk: A Seminar Series. IIASA-CP-82—S2. Laxenburg, Austria: International Institute for Applied Systems Analysis, 1982.

Viek, C., and Stallen, D. J. "Judging Risks and Benefits in the Small and in the Large." Organizational Behavior and Human Performance 18 (1981):235-271.

von Winterfeldt, D., John, R. S., and Borcherding, K. "Cognitive Components of Risk Ratings." Risk Analysis 1 (1981):277-287.

von Winterfeldt, D., and Edwards, W. Decision, Analysis and Behavioral Research. New York: Cambridge University Press, 1986.

Weinstein, N. D. "Why It Won't Happen to Me: Perceptions of Risk Factors and Susceptibility." *Health Psychology* 3 (1984):431-457.

Weinstein, N. D. "Seeking Reassuring or Threatening Information about Environmental
Cancer. *Journal of Behavioral Medicine* (1979):125-139.

Wellborn, S. *The Potential of Mediation for Resolving Environmental Disputes Related
to Energy Facilities*. DOE/EV/10274-1. American Management Systems, 1979.

Speakers' Biographies

Frederick W. Allen, associate director of the Office of Policy Analysis of the U.S. Environmental Protection Agency (EPA), has been with the EPA since 1978. Prior to his present position, he was acting director of the Energy Policy Division, chief of the Energy Policy Branch, and staff director of the Interagency Resource Conservation Committee. Mr. Allen has also worked on the staff of the U.S. secretary of labor, the Federal Energy Administration, the Cost of Living Council, and VISTA. He holds a B.A. from Yale University and an M.B.A. from Harvard Business School.

Alvin L. Alm became chairman of the board and chief executive officer of Thermo Analytical Corporation in 1985, having previously held the position of deputy administrator of the U.S. Environmental Protection Agency for two years. Prior to that, he was director of the Harvard Energy Security Program and assistant secretary for policy and evaluation in the U.S. Department of Energy. He holds a B.A. from the University of Denver and an M.P.A. from Syracuse University.

Etcyl H. Blair, former vice-president and director of health and environmental sciences for the Dow Chemical Company, was with that firm from 1951 to 1986. He is active in the American Chemical Society and the American Association for the Advancement of Science and served as chairman of the Board of Directors for the Chemical Industry Institute of Toxicology. Dr. Blair has been awarded over 20 patents in the field of organophosphous chemistry and is the author of numerous publications. He holds an A.B. from Southwestern College in Winfield, Kansas, and a M.S. and Ph.D. from Kansas State University.

Jackson Browning has been vice-president for health, safety, and environmental affairs at Union Carbide Corporation since 1976, having been with the company for several years before assuming that position. Dr. Browning is on the Board of Directors and Executive Committee of the American Industrial Health Council and is a member of the Health and Safety Committee of the Chemical Manufacturers' Association. He received a B.S. and an LL.B. from the University of West Virginia.

Thomas Burke is the assistant commissioner of the Division of Occupational and Environmental Health within the New Jersey Department of Health. Prior to his appointment to the Department of Health, Dr. Burke was the director of the Office of Science and Research within the New Jersey Department of Environmental Protection. He acted as a science advisor to the commissioner, Department of Environmental Protection, on a broad range of scientific and environmental policy issues. Previous to his appointment as director in 1980, he served as a research scientist with the department. Dr. Burke also serves as a cochairman of the Epidemiology Curriculum Committee for the University of Medicine and Dentistry of New Jersey, Robert Wood Johnson Medical School; a commissioner on the New Jersey Commission on Cancer Research; and a member of the Integrated Environmental Management Subcommittee, which is an Environmental Protection Agency Science Advisory Board. In addition, he is a frequent lecturer on environmental science and epidemiology. Dr. Burke received his doctorate in environmental epidemiology from the University of Pennsylvania, received his masters in public health from the University of Texas, and his bachelor's degree from St. Peter's College in Jersey City, New Jersey.

Vincent T. Covello is the director of the Risk Assessment Program at the National Science Foundation in Washington, D.C. Prior to his joining the Foundation in 1979, he was a study director at the National Academy of Sciences, a professor at Brown University, and a Peace Corps volunteer in Nepal. Dr. Covello received his Ph.D. from Columbia

University and his B.A. with honors and M.A. from Trinity Hall College, Cambridge University, England. He has received numerous awards, including a Woodrow Wilson Fellowship and several government awards for outstanding service. Dr. Covello has authored or edited over 14 books and numerous articles on various aspects of health and environmental risk assessment and management. He has also chaired or cochaired over 20 international conferences on risk assessment, including several NATO Advanced Study Institutes. Dr. Covello is currently the president-elect of the Society for Risk Analysis and serves on the editorial boards of several journals.

Lewis Crampton has been executive director of the National Institute for Chemical Studies since 1984. Prior to that he was director of the Office of Management Systems and Evaluation at the U.S. Environmental Protection Agency (EPA), assistant regional administrator of EPA's Region 5 in Chicago, and commissioner of the Massachusetts Department of Community Affairs. He holds a B.A. from Princeton University, an M.A. from Harvard University, and a Ph.D. from the Massachusetts Institute of Technology.

J. Clarence Davies, executive vice-president of The Conservation Foundation since 1976, is an authority on environmental research and public policy. Before joining the Foundation, Dr. Davies was a fellow with Resources for the Future and, before that, a senior staff member of the Council on Environmental Quality. The author of *Politics of Pollution* and *Neighborhood Groups and Urban Renewal*, and the coeditor of the first edition of *Business and Environment: Toward Common Ground*, Dr. Davies has also been an assistant professor at Princeton University and an examiner at the Bureau of the Budget (now the Office of Management and Budget). He serves on numerous advisory boards. As a consultant to the President's Advisory Council on Executive Organization, Dr. Davies helped draft the reorganization plan that created the U.S. Environmental Protection Agency. He has a B.A. from Dartmouth and a Ph.D. from Columbia University.

Vernon N. Houk is director of the Center for Environmental Health, Centers for Disease Control (CDC), and assistant administrator, Agency for Toxic Substances and Disease Registry in Atlanta, Georgia. He was appointed assistant surgeon general in 1985. Prior to joining CDC in 1968, Dr. Houk was with the U.S. Navy, holding various posts at the Veterans Administration Hospital in Houston, Texas, and the U.S. Naval Hospital in St. Albans, New York; he also was Officer in Charge and Medical Officer at the South Pole Station, Antarctica. A recipient of the 1985 Public Health Service Distinguished Service Medal as well as numerous other awards, Dr. Houk was educated at San Jose State College, the University of California, and the George Washington University School of Medicine, where he received his M.D.

Reed Johnson received his Ph.D. in economics in 1974 from the State University of New York at Stony Brook. He has been a faculty member at Illinois State University, Simon Fraser University, Linkoping University, and the Stockholm School of Economics. Dr. Johnson has been a Brookings Economic Policy Fellow and has received two Fulbright-Hayes fellowships to Sweden. He has published a number of articles on environmental economics and is presently a project officer for an Environmental Protection Agency study on communicating risks to homeowners about indoor radon pollution. He is currently associate professor of economics at the U.S. Naval Academy and an economist in the Office of Policy Analysis, U.S. Environmental Protection Agency.

Roger Kasperson is a member of the Hazard Assessment Group at Clark University's Center for Technology, Environment, and Development (CENTED). From 1977 to 1983, he served as a member of the National Research Council's Board of Radioactive Waste Management and chaired its panel on Social and Economic Issues in Siting Nuclear Waste Repositories. For the past seven years, he has directed a series of research projects funded by the National Science Foundation and the Russell Sage Foundation dealing with technological risk management, industrial management of hazards, and ethical issues involved in risk management. Currently he is working on issues related to emergency planning around nuclear power plants and to siting radioactive and other hazardous waste facilities.

Joanne Kauffman, instructor in international environmental policy at Tufts University, is a consultant on environmental policy and risk communication. She is the former deputy commissioner for policy and communications of the Massachusetts Department of Environmental Management (1983-87). Prior to that, she was a consultant and administrator in the Environment Directorate of the Organization for Economic Cooperation and Development (OECD) in Paris, France. Ms. Kauffman has also been a press assistant in the U.S. House of Representatives; a reporter and editorial assistant for the Vance Publishing Corporation in Chicago, Illinois; and a free-lance writer and researcher. She holds a B.A. from Bradley University and a certificate of European studies from the Institute for American Universities, Aix-en-Provence, France.

Stephen Klaidman, senior research fellow with the Kennedy Institute of Ethics of Georgetown University, is an associate of the Institute for Health Policy Analysis, also at Georgetown University. Prior to this, he was a reporter and deputy foreign editor of *The Washington Post*, news editor and chief editorial writer for the *International Herald Tribune*, and a commentator for WJLA-TV, the ABC affiliate in Washington. Mr. Klaidman is coauthor with Tom Beauchamp of *The Virtuous Journalist*.

Frances Lynn is a senior research associate at the Institute for Environmental Studies at the University of North Carolina (UNC) at Chapel Hill. She directs the Environmental Resource Project, which provides technical assistance and training on environmental issues to community groups and local governments. She is also a research assistant professor in the Department of Environmental Sciences and Engineering at UNC's School of Public Health. In the latter role, she is directing a National Science Foundation Grant on the use of scientific and technological information by senior decision makers in the federal government and private industry. Her other ongoing research includes a study of citizen involvement in the permitting and siting of risky technologies as well as the process of decision making for risk assessments. Previously she taught political science at the undergraduate level, was a senior staff member of the Caroline Brown Lung Association, and a senior research associate at the Systems Research Development Corporation. She holds a B.A. from Goucher College, an M.A. from Columbia University, and a D.P.H. from the University of North Carolina.

David McCallum holds a B.Sc. in chemical engineering from North Carolina State University and an M.S. in chemical engineering and a Ph.D. in biomedical engineering from the University of Virginia. Dr. McCallum has worked for Procter and Gamble, Inc.; the state of South Carolina; the National Heart, Lung, and Blood Institute; and the Office of Technology Assessment of the U.S. Congress. He joined the staff of the Institute for Health Policy Analysis, Georgetown University Medical Center, in 1984. He is a senior fellow and directs the institute's activities in health-risk communication. He is also an assistant professor of community and family medicine.

Alan McGowan has been president of the Scientists' Institute for Public Information in New York since 1974. Previously he served as scientific administrator of the Center for the Biology of Natural Systems at Washington University in St. Louis; as program director of the Water Pollution Project at the Tilton School, New Hampshire; and as adjunct instructor of physical sciences at Pace University in New York. He also spent nine years as a science teacher in secondary schools and two years as an engineer with the American Electric Power Service Corporation in New York. Mr. McGowan is executive editor of *Environment* magazine and a member of the New York State Energy Research and Development Authority. He holds a B.E. from Yale University and was enrolled in the Tufts University Master of Science Institute for Teachers of Science and Mathematics.

Robert C. Mitchell, a sociologist, has been a senior fellow since 1976 with Resources for the Future, a nonprofit research organization founded in 1952 with the assistance of the Ford Foundation to conduct studies of resource, energy, and environmental issues. Previously he was associate professor at Pennsylvania State University, assistant/associate professor at Swarthmore College, and acting assistant professor at Vanderbilt University. Dr. Mitchell is the author of numerous articles and publications on the sociology of environmental and energy issues. He holds a B.A. from the College of Wooster, Ohio, an M.Div. from Union Theological Seminary, and M.A. and Ph.D. degrees from Northwestern University.

Frank Press has been president of the National Academy of Sciences since 1981. Previously, he served for four years as the President's Science Advisor and director of the Office of Science and Technology Policy in the Carter administration. From 1965 to 1977, he was head of the Department of Geology and Geophysics (now the Department of Earth and Planetary Sciences) at the Massachusetts Institute of Technology. He has also served as professor of geophysics at the California Institute of Technology and as director of its Seismological Laboratory. Dr. Press has served several U.S. presidents in advisory capacities and is the recipient of numerous awards. He received a B.A. degree from the City College of New York and advanced degrees in geophysics from Columbia University.

William Ruckleshaus joined the law firm of Perkins Cole in Seattle, Washington, in 1985. He has served twice as administrator of the U.S. Environmental Protection Agency, first when it was formed in 1970 until 1973 and again from 1983 to 1985. Mr. Ruckelshaus has also been acting director of the Federal Bureau of Investigation and deputy attorney general of the U.S. Department of Justice. In 1976, he joined the Weyerhaeuser Company in Tacoma, Washington, as senior vice-president for law and corporate affairs. From 1974 to 1976, he was a senior partner in the Washington, D.C., law firm of Ruckelshaus, Beveridge, Fairbanks, and Diamond. Mr. Ruckelshaus serves as a director of several corporations and is on the board of several organizations, including The Conservation Foundation and World Wildlife Fund. He is also the U.S. representative on the United Nations World Commission on Environment and Development. He holds a B.A. from Princeton University and an LL.B. from Harvard University.

Peter M. Sandman is professor of journalism at Cook College, Rutgers University. Prior to joining the faculty in 1977, he taught journalism and natural resource programs at the University of Michigan, Ohio State University, California State College, and Stanford University. He has served in many advisory capacities at various institutions, including as consultant on communications for the President's Commission on the Accident at Three Mile Island. He has numerous articles and papers to his credit and has received several awards for his work. He received a B.A. from Princeton University and an M.A. and Ph.D. from Stanford University.

Claudine Schneider was elected in 1980 to the U.S. House of Representatives, where she serves on several committees, including Merchant Marine and Fisheries, Science and Technology, and the Select Committee on Aging. Representative Schneider is also cochair of the new Congressional Caucus on Competitiveness and serves on the advisory committee of the Congressional Clearinghouse on the Future. Prior to her election, she was a producer and host of a public affairs program on a Rhode Island NBC affiliate for two years and executive director of the Conservation Law Foundation from 1973 to 1978. She is also the founder of the Rhode Island Committee on Energy. She received a B.A. from Windham College, Vermont.

Ellen Silbergeld has been a senior scientist with the Environmental Defense Fund since 1982. Previously she was a research scientist at the Johns Hopkins School of Public Health and at the National Institutes of Health. She is a guest scientist at the University of Maryland Medical School and a member of the U.S. Environmental Protection Agency's Science Advisory Board and the National Academy of Sciences' Board on Toxicology. Dr. Silbergeld has published over 150 scientific papers; her main interests are toxicology and risk assessment. She received an A.B. from Vassar and a Ph.D. from Johns Hopkins University.

Paul Slovic is with Decision Research, a branch of Perceptronics (Oregon), which he cofounded in 1976. Prior to that, he was with the Oregon Research Institute for 12 years. His fields of specialization are judgment, decision making, and risk assessment, and he has written numerous articles on these topics. Dr. Slovic has been a council member of the Society for Risk Analysis and served as president of the society in 1983 and 1984. He received a B.A. from Stanford University and a Ph.D. from the University of Michigan.

Lee M. Thomas was named administrator of the U.S. Environmental Protection Agency (EPA) by President Reagan in January 1985, succeeding William D. Ruckelshaus. During an 18-year career, Mr. Thomas has served in management positions at all levels of government—federal, state, and local. Throughout the 1970s, he managed statewide criminal justice planning, emergency management, and public safety programs for three consecutive South Carolina governors. In 1981, Mr. Thomas was appointed associate director of the Federal Emergency Management Agency (FEMA) for State and Local Programs and Support. In that position, he was responsible for federal disaster relief, civil defense, and other emergency response programs. In 1982, he became executive deputy director of FEMA. In February 1983, Mr. Thomas became assistant administrator of the EPA in charge of hazardous waste programs. He also served as acting deputy administrator of the EPA from March until August 1983. Mr. Thomas is a graduate of the University of the South and holds a masters degree from the University of South Carolina.

Tom Vacor, consumer journalist and attorney, has been consumer reporter with KCBS-Los Angeles since May 1985, having previously been with a San Francisco TV station. In addition to several years in broadcasting, Mr. Vacor was a consumer affairs executive in the auto industry from 1973 to 1978 and has worked for consumer advocate Ralph Nader. Mr. Vacor holds a J.D. from the Cleveland-Marshall College of Law.

Detlof von Winterfeldt is an associate professor of systems science at the Institute of Safety and Systems Management of the University of Southern California. His research interests are in decision and risk analysis. He is currently the principal investigator for two National Science Foundation/Environmental Protection Agency-sponsored research projects on risk communication.